Kenz

LETTERS HOME

BY

W. D. HOWELLS

AUTHOR OF

"LITERARY FRIENDS AND ACQUAINTANCE"
"LITERATURE AND LIFE" "THE KENTONS"
"THEIR SILVER WEDDING JOURNEY"
ETC. ETC.

NEW YORK AND LONDON
HARPER & BROTHERS PUBLISHERS
1903

LETTERS HOME.

LETTERS HOME.

——◆——

I.

From Mr. Otis Binning *to* Mrs. Walter Binning,
Boston.

New York, *Dec. 12, 1901.*

My Dear Margaret:

I am afraid it will not do, and that you will have your brother-in-law back on your hands again, for the winter, or lose him indefinitely. I do not mean, lose him to New York; far from that; as far as Europe, in fact; for if I were to take stock (the local commercialism instantly penetrates one's vocabulary) of my emotions, I suspect I should find myself evenly balanced between the impulse to board the next train for Boston and the impulse to board the next steamer for Liverpool. The things are about equally simple: the facilities for getting away from New York compensate for the facilities for getting to New York; and I could

1

keep my promise of amusing your invalid leisure by
letter as well from one place as from another.   Wherever I am to be, I am not to be pitied as one taxed
beyond his strength in keeping a rash promise.   Your
rest-cure may be good for you, or it may not; but for
me I am sure it will be good if it gives me back that
boon period of life, when I wrote letters willingly and
wrote them long. I have already a pleasing prescience
of an earlier time; in the mere purpose of writing
you, I feel the glow of that charming adolescence of
the world, in the eighteenth century, when everybody,
no matter of what age, willingly wrote such long letters as to give the epistolary novel a happy air of
verisimilitude.

I wish I could be more definite as to the reasons of
my doubts whether I shall stay here or not. Certainly
the meteorological conditions have nothing to do with
the matter.   Up to the present date these have been
the greatest amiability.   About Thanksgiving there
were some days of rough cold, which with our native
climate still in my nerves, I expected to last for a
week at least; but with the volatility of the New York
nature, it all blew away in forty-eight hours.   The
like has happened several times since; a sort of cor-
rupt warmth has succeeded the cold, affecting one as

if the tissues of the season had broken down through sympathy with the municipal immorality. I should like to stay, if for nothing else, to see what the reformers will do in the way of an honest climate after they get into power at the end of the year, but I do not know whether I shall be able to do it. In the meantime, I like the mildness, though I can never get over my surprise at it; I enjoy it, as I suppose I should enjoy standing in with Tammany, in some enormously wicked deal that turned over half the streets to me for, say, automobile speedways. I had really forgotten what a Florentine sky New York often has in mid-December, by night and by day, with a suffusion of warm color from the sunsets, which is as different from the shrill pink of our Back Bay sunsets as the New York relaxation is from our moral tension. You have been here much later and oftener than I, and I dare say you take for granted all the unseasonable gentleness which I am finding so incredible, and so acceptable. But as yet I am not accustomed to it, and I have a bad conscience in celebrating it.

The whole place is filthier, with the pulling down and building up, the delving for the Rapid Transit, and I do not know what else, than I have seen it since poor Waring first taught Father Knickerbocker (as their newspaper cartoonists like to figure the city), the novelty of purging and living cleanly like a gentleman. and I suppose it is the sense of the invasive, pervasive dirt that has much to do with my doubt whether I can stand it. Now and then a rain comes and washes it all away, and makes the old sloven look *endimanché*, but the filth begins again with the first week day, and you go about with your mouth and eyes full of malarious dust, as you did before. Of course, you will remind me that Boston is always pulling down and building up too ; but her vices whiten into virtues beside New York's in that way. Then the noise, the noise ! All the money from all the stocks and bonds centering their wealth into the place, cannot buy exemption from it. Boston is noisy, too, but there are large spaces in Boston where you can get fairly well away from the noise, and I know of none here, though there is said to be one block up and down next the Riverside Drive which is tolerably free from it; but no one that is any one lives there, for New York is in nothing more anomalous than in having the east side for her fashionable quarter. Everywhere the noise buffets you, insults you ; and the horrible means of transit, that add so much to the danger and the dirt, burst your ears with their din.

I am no longer young, and I am not very well; you are quite right on both of these points; but I am not a dotard quite, or quite an invalid, and I do not exaggerate the facts which you beautiful creatures in your later forties make so light of.   I fancy there is a dreadful solidarity in New York.   I dare not trust myself to the climate, for instance, which I know is doing me good, for fear there is something *behind* it, something colossally uncertain and unreliable, and that later I shall pay with pneumonia for the relief from my nervous dyspepsia.

Just now, indeed, we are in one of those psychological moments when there ought to be great safety for me.   The better element, as it diffidently calls itself, has been given charge of the city, you know, by the recent election, and the experiment of self-government is to be tried once more by people who have apparently so little interest in it.   As nearly as I can make out from chance encounters at the Perennial Club (where Malkin has had me elected a non-resident member; he left town as soon as he had done it), there seems to be what I should call an unexpectation in the general mind: a willingness to take things as they come, to wait on providence in a semi-cynical resignation, which in the last analysis might prove a kind of piety. They have been reformed so frequently, these poor New Yorkers, and then unreformed, that they have rather fallen into the habit of taking the good with the bad as if it might turn out the bad. The newspapers keep shouting away, but that does not count; there are only two or three of them that are ever regarded seriously; and the people at the Perennial, who do not get their politics from London quite so entirely as some of our fellows, are very placid about the municipal situation. They seem to rely altogether on the men who have been put into office, and not the least on those who put them in; in fact the government of New York is almost as personal as that of Germany.

You can read this to Walter; and tell him that the Perennial is certainly a club to be put up at if you *must* come to New York. There are interesting heads, inside and out, here; the house is wonderfully cosy and incredibly quiet, an oasis in a desert of noise; and the windows look out over two miles of woodland in the Park, where I have already begun to take my walks. You will say, Here are the elements of a pleasant sojourn; and I do not deny it; but they are only the elements. The chemistry of their combination is wanting; and what I fear is that at the end of the winter, I should look back over my experience, and find in it nothing but the elements of a pleasant sojourn.

Yours affectionately,

OTIS.

II.

From WALLACE ARDITH *to* A. LINCOLN WIBBERT,
Office of THE DAY, *Wottoma, Iowa.*

NEW YORK, *Dec. 15, 1901.*

Dear Old Linc:

It is simply glorious, there is no other word for it. I have to keep pinching myself, to make sure that it is not some other fellow; but if it be I as I hope it be, I've a little Linc at home, and he'll know me—or words to that effect.   So I will try to sober down and make the appeal to you.   But I feel that it is an awful waste of time, for the subjects crowd upon you here, and what I give to friendship I take from literature. I want you to appreciate that.

It seems strange that it should be only three nights ago that I parted from you with that awful wrench in the dirty old depot at Wottoma, and took the sleeper for Chicago.   Aeons of experience, swept down by deluges of emotion, have passed since then, and I feel

8

older than the earth. I do not think I was very young then; I had gone through what is supposed to age a man, and if it had not been for you, and your sympathy in it all, I do not know what I should have done. But I believe I was wise to wait till I had a better excuse for running away than I had six months ago. I am all right, now, and I am all the better for being at a distance from a Certain Person. If you happen to see her, will you kiss my hand to her, very airily, and say, " *Merci, ma chère*"? If she asks you why, will you tell her that you have heard from W. A., and that his health is perfectly restored? Understand, Linc, I don't blame her now, if I ever did; you will bear me witness that I would not let *you* do it. She had a perfect right to turn me down, but to turn me down for *him*, oh, that *hurt!* I could stand being near her (and yet so far!) but it was being within nose-pulling distance of him that I could not stand. I am glad that I came here to face the ghost down in the midst of men, instead of taking the woods, as I was tempted to do. It would have faced *me* down, if I had gone home, and it would have killed my poor old mother to see my hopeless love-sickness.

That's what I was, Linc: love-sick, and now I am

love-well and it is New York that has completed my
cure. Or rather, she has inspired me with a new passion; she herself is my passion, and I will never leave
to love her evermore! Radiant, peerless divinity, but
majestic and awful too, her splendor dazzles me, her
sovereign beauty enthralls me, her charm intoxicates,
maddens me! What is any mortal girl to this
apotheosis of Opportunity, this myriad-visaged
Chance, this Fortune on a million wheels! There is
more material in a minute here, Linc, than there is in
Wottoma in a year. I don't want to go back on the
dear old place— or *to* it, as George Ade said about
Indiana; but there *is* no Wottoma when you think of
New York; it wipes itself from the map, and vanishes
from the gazetteer.

You will never understand why till you come here,
but you will come some day, and then you will know
all about it. I was wishing to-night when I came out
of the little French restaurant where I dine (it was
the first time, but I am always going to dine there)
that you could have been here to put your hand in
mine, and walk up Broadway with me, just for one
breath, one glimpse of it all. You would not have
needed that dinner—six courses, with wine included,
for fifty cents—warm under your waistcoat, to make

you feel yourself not merely a witness of the great procession of life, but a part of it. By that time every one's work is over, and the people are streaming to the theatres, past the shining shops on foot, and cramming the trolleys, the women in furs and diamonds, and the men in crush hats and long overcoats, with just enough top buttons open to betray the dress tie and dress shirt. (I have laid in one of those majestic overcoats already, and I have got a silk hat, and I would like to show it to you in Wottoma, where you can't buy a silk hat unless you send to Chicago for it.) At the doors of the theatres, more gorgeous women and more correct men are getting out of hansoms, and coupés, and automobiles, and trailing in over the pavements between rows of resplendent darkeys in livery; and life is worth living.

But when I begin anywhere on New York, I want to leave off and begin somewhere else, for the job is always hopeless. Take the Christmas streets alone, at three o'clock in the afternoon, and if you have a soul in you it soars sky-scraper high at the sight of the pavements packed with people, and the street jammed with cars, wagons, carriages, and every vehicle you can imagine, and many you can't, you poor old provincial! I ache to get at it all in verse; I want to write the Epic of New York, and I am going to. I would like to walk you down Twenty-third Street, between Fifth and Sixth avenues, and wake you up to the fact that you have got a country. Only you would think you were dreaming; and it *is* a dream. What impresses me most is the gratis exhibition that goes on all the time, the continuous performance of the streets that you could not get for money any where else, and that here is free to the poorest. In fact, is *for* the poor. There is one window on Fourteenth Street where the sidewalk is a solid mass of humanity from morning till night, entranced by the fairy scene inside; and most of the spectators look as if they had not been to breakfast or dinner, and were not going to supper. But they are enraptured; and that is the great secret of New York; she takes you out of yourself; she annihilates you and disperses you, and you might starve to death here without feeling hungry, for your mind wouldn't be on it. That is what convinces me that I have come to the best place for that little heart-cure.

This afternoon I was in the Park; my hotel is only a few blocks below it, and the woods called to me across the roofs, and I went. The sunset was dying over the Seventh Avenue entrance as I went in and as

I tramped up past a big meadow where they pasture a flock of sheep, and crossed a bridge to a path that follows the border of a lake into what they call the Ramble, far from hoofs and wheels. The twilight was hovering in the naked tree tops, but the sunset was still reflected from the water among the trunks below, and just as I got to a little corner under the hill where there is a bust of Schiller on a plinth, between evergreens that try to curtain it, the red radiance glorified a pair of lovers tilting on the air above the path before me. He had his arm across her shoulders, and she had hers flung round his waist; I stopped, for I felt myself intruding, and that made them look round, and they started apart. Then, after they had taken a few steps, she closed upon him again, and with an action of angelic defiance, as if she said, " I don't care; suppose we are ? " she flung her slim little arm round him, and ran him up the slope of the path past the bust, and round a rock out of sight. It was charming, Linc, but it made me faint, and I dropped down on a bench beside an old fellow who might have been a fellow-sufferer, though he didn't look it. He was got up in things that reduced mine to an average value of thirty cents, and I saw that if I really meant business I must have a pair

of drab gaiters inside of the next twenty-four hours.
I don't know what made me think he was also literary, but I did, and I was flattered to have him speak to
me after he had given me a glance over the shoulder
next me, through his extremely polite *pince-nez*. He
was clean shaven, except for the neat side whiskers, of
the period of 1840–60, as you see them in the old
pictures; and very rosy about the gills, with a small,
sweet smile. You could see that he was his own
ideal of a gentleman, and he looked as if he had been
used to being one for several generations; at least,
that was the way I romanced him; and perhaps that
was why I felt flattered when he suggested, as if I
would perfectly understand, " That was rather pretty. "
I ventured to answer, " Yes, very pretty, indeed. " I
was just thinking how old Schiller would have liked
to wink the other eye of his bust there, and tell them
he knew how it was himself. So I quoted—

> " Ich habe genossen das irdische Glück,
> Ich habe gelebt und geliebet. "

My quotation seemed to startle the old fellow, and
he said " Ah! " and faced around at me, and asked with
an irony that caressed, " Made in Germany ? " I made
bold to answer, " The verses were. I was made in
Iowa." Then I felt rather flat, for having lugged in

my autobiography, but he did not mind, or if he did, he only laughed, and remarked, " A thing like that would make a nice effect on the stage, if you could get it in. " " But you could'nt, " I said, "you could only get it into a poem. It would be gross and palpable on the stage. " " Was it gross and palpable here ? " " No, here it was the real thing. " " I don't see the logic of your position, " he said. " I don't know that I could show it to you. It's something you must feel. " He laughed again, with the revelation of some very well-dentistried teeth, and said, " Well, let's hope that some time I may be fine enough to feel it. If I put it on the stage will it spoil it for a poem? " " Not if I get it into a poem first. " " I shouldn't object to that; I could dramatize the poem. Or perhaps you could. " He got up, and made me a beautiful bow, with his hat off. " We may be rivals, " he said, " but I hope we part friends ? " and I got back with, " Oh, yes, or the best of enemies. "

That made him smile again, and he walked away down the path I had come. He might have been a fine old actor: he had the effect of " going off " at the end of the scene. But think of this happening to me all at once, and out of a clear sky, after the chronic poverty of incident in Wottoma! I suppose

I shall never see him again, but once is enough to enrich the imagination with boundless possibilities. He had an English accent, but I feel sure that he was not English; they study that accent for the stage, of course.

Well, I might as well stop first as last, if this is first; I never should get through; and I should have to dispatch this letter in sections, like a big through train, if it went on much longer. Good-by. I shall not wait for you to write. It would kill me not to write, and you may expect something every day.

Yours ever,

W. Ardith.

P. S.—I shall use that lovers incident in a story. Then I can get my unknown friend in, and I can make use of myself. I see a way to relate our common fortunes to those of the lovers. I believe I can make something out of it. But now I like to let it lie a silent joy in my soul— No, I don't believe I can risk waiting. That old fellow may be going to use the material at once. I believe I shall try making a poem of it, and if I hit it off, I will send you a copy to let you see what I have done with it. If I could only get that thing out as it is in my mind! I think I will imagine some old fellow, seeing in that pair of lovers the phantom of his own love, dead forty years. That would allow me to put in some Thackeray touches, (that elderly unknown was quite a Thackeray type,) and I could use my own experience with a Certain Person. Linc, that girl looked just like a Certain Person: I mean her figure, so slight and light and electrical · and the way she glanced defiantly back at us over her shoulder, when she put her arm round him again!

III.

From ABNER J. BAYSLEY *to* REV. WILLIAM BAYSLEY, *Timber Creek, Iowa.*

NEW YORK, *December 19, 1901.*

Dear Brother :

Yours of the 15th received, and contents noted. Would say that we are all usually well, and getting used to our life here as well as we can. It is worse for wife and I than it is for the girls, but I guess they are a little homesick, too. Am not sure but what it is worse for them, because the girls have not much to do, and mother and me are pretty well taken up, her with her housekeeping, and me getting settled in the business here, and feeling anxious whether I can make it go or not. When the company offered me the place here, at $2,500, I thought it was a fortune, but money does not go quite so far in New York as what it would in Timber Creek; I have to pay forty dollars a month for rent alone, and we live

18

in a six-room flat, with two of the rooms so dark that
we have to burn gas in them by day, and gas costs.
But the kitchen is sunny, and Ma likes that. We
set there of an evening when the girls are carrying on
in the parlor, with their music, and try to make ourselves believe that we are in the old home-kitchen at
Timber Creek; but with a gas range it is difficult.
Was you really thinking of renting the old place?
Would let you have it on easy terms. I can't bear
to think of it standing empty the whole winter long.
Would say, go into it, William, and welcome, for
anything you are a mind to pay. If you didn't
mean that, all right; Ma thought may be you did.
I know your wife would use it well. Would say,
you can have the horse over the winter for his keep,
and if you can sell him for anything in the spring,
will allow you a fair percentage. I know you will do
the best you can for me. Perhaps Watson will take
him off your hands; he wanted a horse.

My, but it brings the old place up to talk about
these things! But a man can't afford to indulge in
much sentiment if he expects to get along in New
York. He has got to be business from the word go.
I try to push things all I can, but sometimes,
William, I am most afraid I am getttng too old for

it, and if the company finds that out it will be all day with me. A trust has no bowels, but I don't blame them, I suppose I should be just so myself. William do you ever think people live too long? There, you will say, he is flying in the face of providence, and the Lord knows I don't mean to, but am thankful for all my blessings. I don't know how ma and the girls could get along without me, old as I am, in this awful city, or me without them for that matter. The girls have not got acquainted much, if any, yet. It is not very sociable here. We have been in this house nearly two weeks, and although as much as twenty families live above and below us, in the six stories, nobody has called. Well its like this, its more like living in the same street than what it is in the same house, but in Timber Creek we wouldn't have been in the same street or hardly in the same town without pretty much everybody calling inside of two weeks. But the girls say they like it, and that it gives them more of a chance to choose their own acquaintance. Speaking of acquaintance, they say that New-Yorkers never meet each other on the street, but if two country fellows happen to be in New York at the same time they are sure to bump against each other before the day's out. And that is just exactly what happened to me this morning in Broadway. You remember the Widow Ardith's boy that went onto the paper in Wottoma? Well, who should I run right into but him day before yesterday, just off the train with his grip in his hand. I told him to come round, and he said he would, the first chance he got, and its fired the girls all up, the idea of a gentleman caller. He always did dress pretty well when he come home from Wottoma on a visit, and he was looking just out of a bandbox, though he never was anyways stuck up. If we could get him for a boarder or to take one of the rooms it would help out considerable, but the girls said they would have my scalp if I dared to hint at such a thing to him, so I am going to lay low. Would say, take the old place William, and if you cannot afford to pay any rent till you have disposed of your house, all right; you can have it for nothing till then. I know you must be uncomfortable where you are, so far from your church, especially evening meetings. You could send us some of the apples. One of them old Rambos or Sheeps Noses would taste good. Ma and the girls joins me in love to you and Emmeline. When you write give our love to the rest of your family. I hope Sally is getting along all right.

To think of you being a grandfather before me when so much younger, but so it goes.

Your affectionate brother,

AB.

IV.

My Dearest Caro:

I owe you a great many apologies for not writing before this, but if you only knew all I have been through you would not ask for a single one. I thought it was bad enough when we got here late in the spring after everybody one knows had gone out of town, but since the season began this fall it has been simply a whirl. It began with the Horse Show, of course, and now we are in the midst of the Dog Show which opened to-day with twelve hundred dogs; and I thought I should go insane with their barking all at once, and when I got mother home, I was afraid she was going to be down ill. But in New York you have got to get used to things, and that is what I keep telling mother, or else go back to Wottoma, where she never put her nose out of the house

23

once in a month, and went to bed every night at
nine. After the Dog Show there will not be much
of anything till the opera begins. Father has taken
a box for the nights when the owner does not go,
and it is going to cost him a thousand dollars for the
time he has it.

We have had a great many cards already, and invitations to Teas and At Homes; they seem to be the
great thing in New York, and I think it is just as
well to begin that way till we know the ropes a little
better. You may be in society all your life in Wottoma, and yet you have got to go slow in New York.
We have been to one dinner at a gentleman's that
father was thrown with in business, but they seemed
to think we did not want to meet anybody but
Western people; and there was nothing about it in
the society column. Father had a good time, for he
always takes his good time with him, and the lady
and her daughter were as pleasant to me as could be ;
mother could not be got to go ; but I did not come to
New York to meet Western people, and I shall think
over the next invitation we get from that house.
They are in the *Social Register*, and so I suppose
they are all right themselves, but if it had not been
for a crowd of people that came in after dinner, I

should not have thought they knew anybody but strangers. I should say nearly all of these after-dinner people were New-Yorkers; there is something about the New York way of dressing and talking that makes you know them at once as far as you can see them. I had some introductions, but I did not catch the names any of the time, and I could not ask for them the way father does, so I did not know who I was talking with.

They all seemed to talk about the theatre, and that was lucky for me, because you know I am so fond of it, and I have been to nearly everything since the season began: Irving, of course, and Maude Adams, and John Drew, and "Colorado," and "Way Down East," and "Eben Holden," and I don't know what all. Father likes one thing and I like another, and so we get in pretty much all the shows. We always take a box, and that gives father practice in wearing his dress suit every night for dinner; I could hardly get him to at first; and he kept wearing his derby hat with his frock coat till I had to hide it, and now I have to hide his sackcoats to keep him from wearing them with his top-hat.

Now, Caro, I know you will laugh, but I will let you all you want to; and I am not going to put on any airs with you, for you would know they were airs the minute you saw them. We do bump along in New York, but we are going to get there all the same, and we mean to have fun out of it on the way. Mother don't because it is not her nature to, like father's and mine. She still thinks we are going to pay for it, somehow, if we have fun, but that is only the New England in her, and does not really mean anything; as I tell her, she was not bred in Old Kentucky, but brown bread and baked beans in Old Massachusetts, and if ever she is born again it will be in South Reading. The fact of it is she is lonely, with father and me out so much, and I am trying to make her believe that she ought to have a companion, who can sit with her, and read to her, and chipper her up when we go out. I need some one myself to write notes for me, and my idea is that we can make one hand wash another by having some one to be a companion for mother who can be a chaperon for me when father cannot go with me. We have advertised, and we shall soon see whether the many in one that we want will appear.

If she will only appear, money will not stand in her way, for we are long on money whatever we are short on. Father is almost as much puzzled in New

York as he was in Wottoma how to spend his in-
come. I am doing my best to show him, and when
we begin to build, in the spring, I guess the architect
will give him some instructions. His plans do more
than anything else to keep mother in good spirits,
and he has made her believe she made them. He
has made father believe he owns him, and I thought
maybe *I* did till he let out one day that there was
some one else. Well, you can't have everything in
this world, and I shall try to rub along.

How would you like to have me rub along with a
cast-off shoe of yours? Not Mr. Ardith! Yes, Mr.
Ardith! He turned up here, last night about dinner
time, and we saw him wandering round with a waiter,
looking for a vacant table, and trying to pretend that
he was not afraid, when any one could see that the
poor boy's heart was in his mouth. The fright made
him look more refined than ever with that clean-
shaven face of his, and his pretty, pointed chin, and
his nice little mouth. He was so scared that he did
not know us, though he was staring straight at us, till
father got up and sort of bulged down on him, and
shouted out, "Well, Wottoma, every time!" And
in about a second, Mr. Ardith was sitting opposite
me, with a napkin across his knees, and talking his

soup cold under the latest news from home. Well,
Caro, it was like some of the old South High Street
times, and it made me homesick to hear all the old
names. And what do you think father did after
dinner? He made Mr. Ardith come up to our rooms,
and the first thing I knew he was asking him how he
would like to go to the theatre with us, if he had
nothing better to do. He made a failure of trying to
think of something, and the next thing I knew,
father was bending over us in the box after the first
act, with a hand on a shoulder apiece of us, (have I
got that straight?) and asking us if we minded his
going, and letting us get home at our convenience.
I looked up and tried to frown him still, but it was
no use. He just said, "I'll send the carriage back
for you, Make, " and went.

I don't believe Mr. Ardith knew there was anything
unusual in it, and I never let on. I hurried up the
talk, and we talked pure literature. I saw I was in
for it, and I tried to make him believe that I had read
all the latest publications, and was taking a course of
George Meredith between times. After while he began to hint round after you, Caro: he did, honest!
He said he supposed I heard from you, and I said,
very rarely; you must be so much taken up with the

Wottoma gayeties. He may have merely asked about you for a bluff, and to show that he was not going to ask. He went on and talked a little more about you, kind of with a ten-foot pole, and getting further and further off all the time, till he got clear to New York, and then he talked about nothing but New York. He is crazy about the place, and sees it as a poem, he says; goodness knows what he means! He got quite up into the clouds, and he did not come down again till we reached home.

I saw that he wanted to do the handsome thing, and I allowed him to order some expensive food at the table we usually take, for I knew that it would hurt his pride if I didn't. He seemed to have a good appetite, but he went on more psychologically than ever, and I was never so glad as when he said good-night to me at our door—except when father wanted him to come in, and he wouldn't. Yes, Caro, Mr. Ardith is too many for me, but I respect him, and if I could scratch up a little more culture perhaps I could more than respect him. He certainly is a nice boy.

We shall probably be at the Walhondia, the whole winter. You see life here, and although it is not exactly the kind of New York life that I am after, it is

New York life, because it's all strangers. I would like you to see it once, and why couldn't you come on and pay me that visit? I would like nothing better than to blow in a few thousand on a show for you, and ask the Four Hundred to meet you. Father would believe they all came, and he would like the blowing-in anyway. He is not going to die disgraced, as Mr. Carnegie says, and he can't die poor if the Trust keeps soaring as it has for the last six months. Better come, Caro, for perhaps when we get into our new house on the East Side next winter, I may not want you, and now I *do* want you. Come! I'll give a little theatre dinner for you, and I'll ask Mr. Ardith. There!

As we used to say when we thought we knew French,

Toute à vous,

MAKE.

New York, December the Eighteenth, Nineteen Hundred and One.

V

From MISS FRANCES DENNAM *to* MRS. ANSEL G. DENNAM, *Lake Ridge, New York.*

NEW YORK, *Dec. 19, 1901.*

Dear Mother :

I have the greatest mind to be like a good girl in a book, and tell you that I have got my ideal place; I know you are so anxious; but I guess I had better not. I am not the least bit discouraged, for I am sure to find it, though it does seem a little too much on the shrinking violet order. When I think of the number of ideal places that I am adapted to, I wonder they can all escape me; and I know I shall run one of them down at last. There are places which I could have got before now if I had not set my mark so high. Only yesterday I was offered a situation as hello-girl at a telephone station, and I could be sitting this moment with the transmitter at my mouth, and

the receivers strapped to both ears, and looking as if
I were just going to be electrocuted, if I had chosen.

Perhaps I may decide to go into Sunday journalism.
How would you like that—if you knew what it was?
My chum, Miss Hally, is a Sunday journalist, and
perfect bundle of energy. I believe she could work
me in easily. She is from the South, or Soath, as
she calls it, and she is one of these Southern women
you meet here in New York, who make you think
Southern women got so much rest in the old slavery
times, that they never want to rest any more. They
beat us poor Northern things all hollow in getting
places, and the fact is that the only place I've got
yet is the place I live in. That boarding house got
to be a little too much, and before my week was up,
on Wednesday, I began prospecting. Miss Hally
went round with me and it was very well she did,
because it is easier to get out of a tight place if there
are two of you, and to make up flattering excuses,
than it is if there is only one. In New York you
have to be so careful—you have no idea in Lake
Ridge *how* careful. Whole neighborhoods are barred,
and sometimes when the streets are nice you have to
pass through others that are not; it's horrid. Well,
it all ended, much sooner than we could expect, in

our finding these two rooms, five pair up, in an apartment with respectable people who are glad to let them, and let us get breakfast in their kitchen. We go out for our lunches and dinners to a French boarding-house in the neighborhood, where the food is wonderful and the men all smoke cigarettes at the table; but they do not mean anything by it. Our rooms look south over a beautiful landscape of chimneys, and it is astonishing how all chimneys seem to be out of order and have to have something done to them; there is not a perfectly well chimney as far as the eye can reach. One room we use as a parlor, and the other has two let-down beds in it, and both are full of sun. It is delightful, and I know things are going to turn out just as I wish, for if you wish hard enough they have got to.

You mustn't fret, or else I shall come home and shake you. My hundred dollars will last three months, or I will know the reason why. I think I will advertise, and get Miss Hally to go over the answers with me, and tell me which ones I had better follow up. She knows New York through and through, and if any one can help me run down my ideal employer she can. I have not swerved from a single requirement: age, amiability, opulence, with an

eye on Europe in the spring. She will not have much
for me to do : just notes to write, accounts to keep,
friends to receive and excuse her to, reading aloud in
the evenings, with a perfectly ridiculous consideration
for my strength, because I am long and rather limp and
slab-sided, and must be sick; I shall have to overcome her fears for my health before she will consent
to take me even on trial, and nothing but something
strangely fascinating in me will help me to win the
day. The only condition she will make is that I shall
pay you a good long visit in May, before we sail.
Perhaps she will let me begin it before, if she sees I
am homesick, which I shall not be, and you needn't
think it. But I suppose the sunset still has that bur-
nished crimson through the orchard and over the lake,
and the Ridge woods are all red in it, and the vine-
yards black—how purple they were with grapes when
I left! The chickens have gone to roost in the peach
trees, and the guinea-hens are trying to make up their
minds to, and you are standing by the gate looking
wistfully down to the desolate depot for your run-
away girl, and wondering how she is. She is very,
very well, mum, and she is coming home with a
pocketful of money to pay off that mortgage. But
if you stand there at the gate, looking that way,

mother, you will break my heart! Go in, this minute, or you will take cold, and then what shall I do? Give my love to all inquiring friends—very nasal love, and not sweeter than you can conscientiously make it. Then the neighbors will know that it is honest. Love to Lizzie, and tell her to be very good to you.

Your affectionate daughter,

FRANCES.

VI.

From Miss Frances Dennam *to* Mrs. A. G. Dennam, *Lake Ridge.*

New York, *December 26, 1901.*

Dear Mother:

I was disappointed yesterday in not getting that ideal place to send you for a Christmas present. It would have been so nice, that I thought surely I should get it; but you must not lose faith in me, for I confidently expect it this week, and you shall have it on New Year's at the latest. I may have to telegraph it; but you will not mind that. The truth is the day has been so exciting that I did not grieve much for the ideal place, and my disappointment was mostly for you, because I had promised you. I was almost entirely taken up with my chum, Miss Hally, who told me, when we were both in the melting mood of clawing the candies out of each other's stockings, where we had put them the night before, all about

36

herself, and now I will tell you: I forgot to before.
She is Miss Custis Hally, and she says her father
was always opposed to slavery, and would not go
with the rest when Virginia seceded, but just stayed
on his plantation and took no part in the war. Miss
Hally came to New York, after he died, and has
worked on a newspaper here, ever since. She has got
one of the best places now, but I guess it has been a
fight. She is only forty, but her hair is as white as
snow. She is tall and straight, and beautiful, with a
kind of fierceness in her looks, that all breaks up
when she speaks of anything she pities, and she has
been kinder to me than I could ever tell you, though
some day I will try. She has taken my case in hand,
and you can count upon getting that place from me
on New Year's without fail, for I have begun to have
answers to my advertisement already. None of them
are just what I wanted, but it is a good deal for some
of them to be what I can get. I needn't tell you
about them till I have gone over them with Miss
Hally. She is going to help me boil them down to-
night, and I will start out with the residuum to-
morrow, and see which I will take. This sounds
rather majestic, but it is not as majestic as it sounds.
I have only got two answers that seem honest; the

rest are fakes of one kind or another, to get money out of me; I can see that for myself; but I depend upon Miss Hally to advise me about these two. You will soon hear from me, if I have luck, and if I haven't you won't hear so soon.

Your gift and Lizzie's came this morning, a day after the fair, which reopened on account of them. I was afraid you were going to forget me, and when you hadn't, I wished you had. When I think of your using up your poor old eyes on that collar for me, I feel like giving you a good scolding for making me cry. Lizzie's book-mark is beautiful, and when I get to reading aloud to the Unknown Lady that I am going to be companion to, I won't use any other. I shall have the collar on, and she will try to beg them both of me, but of course I will be quite up and down with her. Good-by, you dear ones!

Your loving daughter and sister,

FRANCES.

VII.

From WALLACE ARDITH *to* A. L. WIBBERT,
Wottoma.

NEW YORK, *Dec. 18, 1901.*

My dear Lincoln:

I do not want to crowd you with personal intelligence, but I shall not sleep to-night unless I tell
someone that I have spent the evening with our old
friends, the Ralsons, or rather our young friend, *the*
Ralson.

The people at Lamarque's would no more think of
dressing for dinner than the most exclusive club men
of Wottoma (if there were any,) but to-night I had
the ambition to see how much a poor young man
could dine for at the Walhondia and that was why I
was all right as to clothes when I wandered into the
glittering banquet hall, and found the Ralsons there.
I knew they lived at the Walhondia, and I thought I
might stumble on them, but when I did, I was able

to give a good imitation of never being so much surprised in my life.   The old gentleman had me down
at their table in less time than I can tell it; and after
dinner, before I knew it, he had me at the theatre
with himself and America; and then as suddenly, as
things happen in dreams, I was there alone with her.
She seemed to think it tremendously exciting, being
left with me in their box; and she treated her
father's abandoning us, on pretence of seeing a man
somewhere after the first act, with a severity that
slipped from her in one of those fine, large yawps of
hers.   She said, "O well, we're all Wottoma inno-
cents together, and nobody knows us, anyway, " and
I could pass for her cousin, if not her mother or aunt,
or some other elderly relative; and I realized that she
was referring to the chaperonage that we are always
reading about.   After that we proceeded to have a
good time, though we put up an icy front, that struck
a chill to the beholder, whenever we found people
looking at us.

They looked at us a good deal, and I didn't wonder, for America is certainly beautiful to look at.
Of course that hair of hers excites suspicion, but a
woman has only got to behave as if she believed a
thing was real herself, and she carries conviction.   I

could see doubt fade from the opera glasses of the ob-
servers at the theatre, and from their eyes at supper afterwards (I blew in about five dollars for a few gilded
morsels, when we got back to the hotel), as they settled down to perfect faith in her particular rich
mahogany shade of hair and gave themselves up to
the joy of her sumptuous bloom and bulk, as something that there could never have been any question
about. She was the handsomest girl in the theatre
and the handsomest in the supper room, and she did
not go half way down her spine to prove it, as some
of the women did. I always did think her red, white
and blue gorgeousness the richest type of beauty, even
when my taste was more for something dark and fine.
We got to talking about my taste at the theatre, after
we had gone over the novel and the drama (she is
more at home in the drama) and I thought it best to
make a few careless inquiries about a Certain Person.
The beauteous America corresponds with a Certain
Person, but she pretended for my comfort that she
had not heard from her for some time. She said she
had asked a C. P. to visit her, and she put on ignorance enough to enable me to promise that I would be
one of a theatre party if the C. P. came.

She said, when we parted at the door of her apartment, that I need not wait to hear that the C. P. was here before calling, and from this and other things that I have put with it, I infer that the divine America's social progress in New York has not been quite equal to her social ambition. I don't mean that she isn't kind hearted enough to wish to make it pleasant for me here, but if she had a great many engagements, I doubt if she would have so much time for a country acquaintance. So far, I should think she had seen New York from her hotel, and that is not the best social basis, I imagine. Her hotel *is* New York, in a certain way, in the way of being a cluster of infinitely repellant particles, as Emerson says, of strangers. But there must be another New York, and I do not believe she has broken into that yet, but this may be because I am so entirely on the outside of it myself. Still I am within guessing distance, and what I guess is that in an old place like this there must be a society so sufficient to itself that it need not be at the pains to be exclusive, and so richly indifferent to what others can bring it that no amount of money can affect its imagination. I have an idea that it might be years before the people of such a society would ever hear of people like the Ralsons. What could people with great-grandfathers in all the old grave-yards here, and with family trees to burn, want with the Ralsons? That is what has begun to steal darkly in upon me from the Ralson situation, and I guess that the divine America, who is as sharp as she is beautiful, knows the facts, and it is to her credit that she has not soured on them. She is as jolly as ever she was, and she is just as determined to make her way as if it were open before her. Perhaps it is, and perhaps I am mistaken.

Perhaps if I lived at the Walhondia I should see things in a different light. I wish on some accounts, if not others, that I did live there, for it is a great world. Simply to sit in the office, and watch the smooth working of the huge machine is to store up impressions for a life-time. The way the clerks, call-boys, and porters operate the arriving and departing guest is so wonderful in itself, that the glimpses of the dining rooms and drawing rooms, and the over-dressed women guests trailing through the corriders, with their underdressed men after them, and the he and she New York swells of all sorts and conditions who come in for supper, (like myself!) are naughti-nesses of superfluity, embarrassments of riches.

But I must stop, merely adding that the Ralsons

took me to and from the theatre in their electric coupé, and America has just sent me home in it! She wished her best regards to you, Linc, and she seems to have a soft place in her spacious heart for all Wottoma.

Yours ever,

W. ARDITH.

VIII.

From WALLACE ARDITH *to* A. L. WIBBERT, *Wottoma.*

NEW YORK, *Dec. 19, 1901.*

My dear Linc:

I have a misgiving that my letter of last night implied a sort of a slight for America Ralson which I certainly do not feel. She has lots of sense, and is as fine as she is frank in the things that become a girl. That is, she is not changed from what you knew, and if anything I wrote gave merely the impression of her physical beauty, it was unfair to her and disgraceful to me. I had no right to speculate about her society prospects even; they may be all she could wish, and still leave her time and place for kindness to me, unworthy. I never liked the Ralson money, but I must say that it seems to crowd my imagination less in New York than it did in Wottoma, and that in old Ralson's civility to me last night I thought there was more personal friendliness

45

than I had realized in him before. He *is* coarse, but he is not hard, and where there is any little question of his being good to his wife or daughter, he is not so coarse as at other times. These are the hasty conclusions of a man who has eaten his canvas-back and drunken his claret, and ridden in his electric. They might not stand the test of greater experience, but though I own that he is the sort of man born to make money, I do not believe he is altogether selfish, or at least that he is incapable of self-sacrifice where his loving, or even his liking lies. If he did not love you or like you no doubt he would be capable of another sort of sacrifice in which he would not figure as the offering.

As yet I do not know how many opportunities I shall have for studying him (he would be great material) for I do not know when I shall be living at the Wolhondia. The humiliating fact is, I have done the very thing I should not have done if I had not been more of an ass than I am willing to allow.

You remember old man Baysley, who used to come from Timber Creek up to Wottoma, in the infant days of Ralson's Trust? Well, he is living now—he would say "residing," and it's hardly living—in New York where he has some employment from the

Cheese and Churn Trust, and is as lonesome as a cat in a strange garret. As luck would have it, he was about the first human being out of two or three millions that I struck against when I got out of my train when I arrived, and he made me promise to come and see " the folks. " At the same time I promised myself that I would not do it, but in about a week I ran across him again and then I was in for it. He took me home with him " to supper "—they dine at twelve o'clock, just as they did in Timber Creek,— and Mrs. Baysley was so pitifully glad to see me, and the girls so proudly glad, that I was rather glad myself. I never really saw much of them at home, though I went to school with the girls when we were children ; but country makes kind, and before I knew it, I was sitting before their radiator with them, swapping reminiscences, and making the old people laugh ; such simple old souls, and so willing to laugh ! The father and mother each confided to me how homesick the other was, and the girls said they did not think New York was half as nice as Timber Creek, to live in, though it would be a great place to come to, for a few weeks in the winter.

When I got up to go, Mrs. Baysley said, now father must show me the flat. But they all followed through it with me—six little boxes of rooms, counting the parlor and the girls' bed-room portiered off it as two. The whole place was furnished with their poor old Timber Creek things citified up, and their home carpets cut into rugs. They took me last into the "spare-room" at the back of the flat, and when the old lady let out that they really had more room than they wanted, for all the place seemed so small, and the old man looked anxious, and the girls hung their heads, the time had come for me to make an ass of myself, and I asked what was the matter with my taking that room. They made some decent demur, but not much, and we agreed on three dollars a week; and here I am, pretty far up on the west side of Central Park, about a block and a half from one of the gates, so that I can get in and meditate the thankless muse, as easily as I could from my hotel, where I was paying seven dollars a week for my room, without the sun, or the view of the neighborhood wash which I have here for less than half the money. The wash hangs from lines supported upon lofty flag staffs, behind the house, and it is very gay ; if we are five flights up, still the halls and stairs are carpeted in a kind of blood-red tapestey brussels the whole way : Mrs. Baysley is very proud of that carpeting, though it is not hers. When I want to get in I touch a bell-button in the vestibule, and they free the latch by a sort of electric arrangement in their flat; but the old man promises me a latch-key when he can get round to it. When I'm late, he sits up and lets me in, and the girls keep breakfast for me long after he has gone down town next morning. I breakfast here, and browse about for lunch and dinner, and accumulate material. Now and then I take a turn at that Central Park incident of the lovers. I have tried it as an idyl, in hexameters, and as a Thackeray ballad, and I have tried it in prose; and it is getting as tough as a piece of bear's meat which the more you chew it the more you can't swallow it. But I don't despair, and won't, as long as you let me sign myself

Your friend,

W. A.

IX.

From MISS FRANCES DENNAM *to* MRS. DENNAM,
Lake Ridge.

NEW YORK, *Jan. 10, 1902.*

Well, mother dear:

I have got it! I've just sent you a telegram, (I
knew they would make you pay fifteen cents for
bringing it up from the station,) so as to take away
the taste of my last two or three gloomy letters as
soon as possible; and now I am going to tell you all
about it. When I told you the failure of those two
places, that I went to look at with Miss Hally, I was
so down-hearted that I hardly knew what to do; I
wanted to give up, and take the first train home, and
try for a school again. But I used all the proverbs I
could put my mind on, and I said my prayer when I
went to bed, just like a little girl, and cried into my
pillow like a big one, and woke the next morning as

bold as brass. I went down town and put in a new advertisement setting forth my gifts and accomplishments, bought all the papers, and read their "wanteds" over my lunch at the Woman's Exchange; and that night I got Miss Hally to go over them with me. We got a good deal of forlorn fun out of it, but not much encouragement, and then Miss Hally proposed a still hunt, as she called it. We put aside two or three selected wanteds that we decided to investigate and see if they were deserving; and Miss Hally said she would begin the still hunt at once, by writing letters to half a dozen different people who might or might not be looking for a prize of my description, and offer them a chance in the raffle. She said this sort of thing would take time, but the results, even if they were failures would be more satisfactory than the other failures we had made. She looked awfully tired, for she had been writing out a long story, as she called it—a biography-interview with a new English lecturess who has just come ashore—but she kindled up at the chance of killing herself for me, and when she put me out for the night she kind of held me off by both shoulders, and then pulled me up and kissed me, for luck, as she said. I was so overcome that I could not even shed a tear; I just gasped, and took it in frozen silence, like a true Lake Ridger.

It seemed to do as well as anything, though, so far as the luck was concerned, I got to thinking afterwards that perhaps it was not the right kind of kiss. The still hunt turned out as badly as the kind of gunning in the newspaper did when I first began to advertise, and when I felt as if everybody could see and hear me. Days, weeks, went by just as they do in novels when the author wants to skip; and yesterday I got word from the public telephone at our corner drug store that there was some one on the wire for me. You can bet, (or you could, if you ever *did*,) that I didn't let the grass grow under my feet, either on the stairs down to the door, or in the street outside. Somehow I just *knew* that this time I was *it*; and sure enough I found it was Miss Hally on the wire. She was calling me from the Hotel Walhondia and she wanted to know if I could come right down. and I said I could come like lightning, and she told me to inquire for Miss Ralson and I would find her there too.

Well, I don't know how I got to the hotel or how I lived through sending my name from the office, and then followed it; but before I wanted to be I was in-

side the Ralson apartment. Of course by that time
I was in my usual frosty calm with strangers; but I
tried to limber up enough to answer Miss Ralson's
questions, and to realize that Miss Hally was going
away and leaving us to each other as soon as the
questions began. She gave me a squeeze of the hand
that said it was all right, and I felt how nice it was
of her not to stay and hear that I wouldn't do if I
happened not to. Miss Ralson was pretty tremendous
at first, and from time to time she was tremendous as
we went on, but every now and then she broke down,
and was not half so awful as I was. I think she saw
that if she was to get at me at all, she would have to
thaw me out to begin with. She asked me whether I
had been to luncheon, and when I made out to
remember I hadn't, she said she thought we could
talk so much better over a little lunch, and she
ordered her maid to order it served to us there; and
all the time she kept on talking, and now and then
breaking into the largest kind of laugh. She has a
head of dark red hair, and the bluest blue eyes, and
white cheeks with soft pink in them, and she is built
on the sky-scraping plan of the new girl, with
shoulders and a neck to beat the band. I have got a
fresh supply of slang from Miss Ralson, for after we

cosied down to the lunch, she talked so much of it that I had to talk it too or seem impolite, and I was not going to do *that*. But she is business, every-time, in spite of her ups and downs of manner, and I can tell you she put me through my paces pretty thoroughly.

She said that they wanted me to be a companion to her mother, and read to her and amuse her any way I could when she and her father could not be at home with her. But they did not want me for that alone; she needed a secretary to write her notes, and keep track of her engagements, and to go with her where a chaperon was not exactly needed, but two girls would do. She asked me if I would just write her a little note, then and there, and say whether I liked the notion, and what salary I should expect; she must have talked that point over with Miss Hally, for she said I could mention twelve hundred if I liked. She put me down at her desk with some note paper, and went away to the window, while I struggled with the note, and she kept coming back to see if I had finished. When I had, she looked pretty hard at it, and compared it with some notes she had received, and then she said, Yes, that would do first-rate. She asked me if I was sure about the spelling, because *she*

always spelt salary with two lls, and she offered to
bet me what I dared that hers was the right way.
We referred it to the dictionary leaves in her porte-
folio, and I won, of course, but we had forgot to say
what we had bet, and so I didn't win anything but
the bet. She seemed perfectly delighted, and she
said that if there was anything she did envy another
person it was spelling; and now she felt sure of me,
if I thought I could get along with her mother.

She took me to her mother in the next room, and
introduced me, and I had a wicked pleasure in seeing
that Mrs. Ralson was more scared than I was. She
is a very small old lady, not the least like her daughter, and she began to question me about where I came
from, and my family, and whether I was homesick,
and didn't I think New York was an awful place. I
agreed to everything, and that seemed to cheer her
up considerably, and she showed me the photograph
of their house in Wottoma, Iowa, where they came
from, and said it was considered the most beautiful
" home " in the place. She pointed out the windows
of her room, which Mr. Ralson had planned for her,
and furnished himself, for a surprise, before she ever
went into it, and she had never changed a thing. It
was before they had formed the Cheese and Churn

Trust, and always expected to live in Wottoma, but afterwards nothing would do America but to come to New York. That was better than Europe, anyway, where they had spent a year; and now Mr. Ralson had *bought*, up between Fifth Avenue and Madison, and they were going to build in the spring, and she supposed they should always live here, but she preferred Wottoma, herself, where you could have some ground around you, and everybody was neighborly.

Well, mother, it made me a little homesick to hear her go on, and I showed that I felt for her, and before we got through, we were old friends, and she said she knew we could get on together first-rate, and she would not work me too hard, and I must not let Make. Make was a good girl, but she was thoughtless, and wanted to be on the go the whole while. She got to talking of Miss Ralson by her nickname, (her whole name is America) and of her husband by his first name, and she was so helplessly humble and simple, that I was glad her daughter had gone out of the room, for I am afraid she would have checked her, and I wouldn't have liked that. Mrs. Ralson is New England born, and I told her you were too, and then she seemed to think I was. I explained how Lake Ridge was settled from New England, and she said that if we were the same kind of people, it came to the same thing.

It is all as different from what I had planned, as could be, but I am not so sorry as I would have supposed. The Ralsons are not an old Knickerbocker family, with stately, highbred ways, and old mahogany sideboards and ancestral silver, but they *will* be, if they live here long enough; and I shall get on with them much better as they are at present. Perhaps an old Knickerbocker family would not have much use for me; and I shall have a better chance to grow up with the country here if I begin with an old Wottoma family. They may rot send me to Europe for my health, but I think they will let me go out to see you in May, about apple-blossom time, with a pocket full of money for the June interest. How thankful I ought to be, and how thankful I am! I am going to do everything I can to deserve my good fortune, and you need not be afraid to hear of my misbehaving! It is all settled that I am to begin earning my salary, with two lls, tomorrow. The arrangement is for me to keep on here with Miss Hally, and not to live with the Ralson's, till they get into their house. When they keep me too late for me to get home alone, they will send me in their automobile or get me a room in the hotel. The way they don't mind money, takes my breath away. After I got through with her mother to-day, Miss Ralson asked me how I would like to go shopping with her a little while, and in about two hours I saw her spend a thousand dollars. She bought anything she fancied, and some things that she didn't fancy, as she found out later. But she said you could always exchange them, and if you couldn't you could get rid of them somehow. It is a great thing to have a Cheese and Churn Trust for a father. I have not seen him, yet, but Mrs. Ralson says Miss Ralson is his "perfect image," and they are just alike, every way.

I feel as if I had not said anything, and were horrid and unthankful, and I don't know what all. But *you* musn't. Tell Lizzie that if she is very, very good, I will let her have some of my old things as soon as I have any new ones.

With best love to you both,

FRANCES.

X.

From WALLACE ARDITH *to* A. L. WIBBERT, *Wottoma.*

NEW YORK, *Jan'y 10, 1902.*

You dear old fellow:

You really mustn't print things from my letters, unless you want to take the frankness out of me. I can't write to all Wottoma as ingenuously as I write to you; I can understand your grief at having my good things wasted on you alone, but I really can't let you share my bounty with the public. If the *Day* people were to ask me for New York letters, and were to offer me decent pay for them, that would be something to consider—and refuse; for I am going to devote myself to pure literature here, at least till I starve at it; and I can't let the *Day* have my impressions for nothing, or next to it.

I wish I had put them down, as I felt them, from moment to moment since I arrived, but perhaps they will be full enough in my letters; of course you will *keep* my letters, and let me recover them as material for my epic, later on. New York gains in epicality every day, and the wonder is that I don't get familiar with it: I get more and more strange. The novelty of it is simply inexhaustible, and the drama of its tremendous being is past all saying. The other day, as I was walking up town after a cup of tea with the sumptuous America at her hotel, I struck into Broadway, and abandoned myself to the spectacle of the laborers digging the foundations for a sky-scraper at one of the corners. They had scooped forty or fifty feet into the earth, below the cellars of the old houses they had torn down, and were drilling into the everlasting rock with steam drills. A whole hive of men were let loose all over the excavation, pitching the earth and broken stones into carts, lifting the carts by derricks to the level of the street, and hitching the horses to them, and working the big steam shovels hanging from the derricks, and the engines were snorting and chuckling and the wheels grinding. and the big horses straining and the men silently shouting at them,—the whole thing muted by the streaming feet of the multitude, and the whine of the trolleys, and the clatter of the wagons, and the crash and roar of the elevated trains; and pretty soon, a mud-covered Italian ran out of the depths with a red flag, and the rest ran to cover, and puff! went a blast that tore up tons of rock, and made no more of a dint in the great mass of noise than if it had been the jet of white vapor that it looked like. Life here is on such a prodigious scale, and it is going on in so many ways at once that the human atom loses the sense of its own little aches and pains, and merges its weakness in the strenuousness of the human mass.

I suppose that is the reason why literature, as a New York interest, affects me less in New York than it did in Wottoma. I know here, as I knew there, that this is a literary centre, and now and then I catch a glimpse of authorship in the flesh. But either because the other interests dwarf the literary interests, or because literature is essentially subjective, it is, so far, disappointingly invisible and intangible. Some of the young fellows dine at Lamarque's, and have a table to themselves in one corner, where they talk and smoke; but I don't know any of them yet, and I haven't quite the gall to make up to them. I suppose there must be literary houses where authors meet; but I have not begun to frequent them, and in my dearth of poets I try to make out with the poem which I find more and more in the personality of the divine America,

In fact, I am seeing a good deal of the Ralsons, these days; or they are seeing a good deal of me. I seem to represent home and mother to Mrs. Ralson, and she claims part of every call I make at the Walhondia for a terribly long talk about Wottoma; though, as for calling, I am mostly there by invitation to all the meals of the day, including supper after the theatre or opera.

America has set up a secretary for herself and a companion for her mother in the single person of a girl from western New York, somewhere, who does duty as a dragon when Ralson is away, or cannot be pressed into the service. She doesn't look like a dragon exactly; in fact, with her shyness and brownness of hair and dress, she makes me think of a quail and its dead-leaf plumage; and she has a way of slipping under cover which I think would not be finally inconsistent with an ability to peck. To tell the truth, as nearly as I can make out on such short notice, the secretary-companion and I were born doubtful of each other; though I should be puzzled to say why. She seems, for reasons of her own, to look with a censorious eye upon America's frank friendliness for me as something very mistakenly bestowed. This naturally puts me on my most cynical behavior;

I say nothing but heartless things in the secretary's presence; and if it goes on I shall turn out a hardened worldling, and be marrying America for her money before I know it. In view of this novel character, I do not understand how it is that the Mayor has not put me on the committee for the reception of Prince Henry. I think I could be guilty of a base servility that would satisfy the secretary's worst expectation.

You must not, by the way, imagine that New York is as hysterical about the prince's visit as the newspapers make her appear. Journalism, my dear Lincoln, I do not mind confiding to you, now I have left it, is feminine; it likes to talk, and to hear itself talk, and it does not mind what the topic is: it can be as shrill and voluble about one thing as another. But I assure you that between the morning and the evening editions, there are long moments when we forget the prince altogether and

"Shouldn't hardly notice it at all,"

in the words of Dockstader's latest song, if he forgot to come.

Yours ever,

W. A.

XI.

From MR. OTIS BINNING *to* MRS. WALTER BINNING,
Boston.

NEW YORK, *Jan. 11, 1902.*

My dear Margaret:

If it surprises you to find this post-marked New York, instead of London, I confess that it rather puzzles me to explain why I have no more taken the steamer for Liverpool than the train for Boston. I can merely say that New York has given me pause, which is the last thing one would expect New York to do. Three weeks ago I might have thought that I knew the place, but now I am not sure that I can more than conjecture it a little bit, or throw out a vague suggestion or two at it. I might analyze accurately enough, but the fancy of synthetizing has grown upon me, and to synthetize New York is impossible.

At least it is impossible for a Bostonian, of the

Boston which, if it was as we believed it, is now certainly no more. We were (forgive the aoristic preterite; it is crueler for me than it is for you!) immensely, intensely, personal, and the note of New York is impersonality. If you wish to lose yourself, this is the shop; if you wish to find yourself, better go somewhere else. Our quality, and the defect of our quality, in that obsolete Boston, was from the wish to find ourselves, always. Here I feel resolved into my elements at times, in a measure which I do not believe would happen to me even in London or Paris. I am mere humanity; worse, I am mere mortality, as some one said of the people in Maeterlinck's little mysteries, and I meet my fellow mortals in a sort of reciprocal dispersal; and yet, when I freely accept the conditions, the experience is rather pleasing. You will not believe it, or at least you will not believe it of me, and you could not acquire faith without coming here and staying rather longer than you are ever likely to do.

It is not that people do not talk of people in New York, but they do not talk of them in our way, as acquaintance from the cradle up, by their nicknames or pet names, with a constant sense of their lurking cousinship. There is of course, this sort of intimacy here, but it does not quite turn the sojourner out of doors. I have been to your Van der Doeses, and they have been hospitable, but they did not make me feel that I mattered. I did not wish to matter, and yet an expectation of that sort ought to be imagined. They were very light, as people of the old Dutch blood are apt to be (the Dutch Calvinism was so very different from our Puritanism!) and though they had the evidences of refinement about them, I had somehow a fear that they might any moment begin asking conundrums. I do not know how else to put it, and I am afraid my meaning will not be perfectly clear to you. Is it possible that there was something in the air of our elder Boston, breathed from the interstellar spaces where our lights of literature and learning, of poetry and philosophy shone so long, which penetrated our psychical substance as nothing of the kind has the New Yorkers'?

One curious experience as a Bostonian has come to me from these New Yorkers through their remote verification of the fact that we Bostonians are no longer so literary or philosophic as we once were. In that former time they imagined us lettered pedants or transcendantal cranks, and they laughed at their notion of us. Now they have somehow (their unintelligence is baffling) caught on to a change in us, and they no longer smile at our queerness; they no longer think of us at all; we suggest nothing to them. This is putting it rather crudely, and it is saying it in excess, of course, but a sad truth lies at the bottom of the well in which I hope this may not make you wish to drown yourself.

At the Van der Doeses' I could naturally meet none but their own kind; but they have been retrospectively more attentive than they actually were, and they have taken me with them to several functions, and had cards sent me for others, where I have seen a greater variety of my fellow mortals. You know I never scorned those simple at-homes and teas which most men disdain, and now when dinners rather take it out of me, I have been going to afternoon receptions with more than my earlier ardor. I have had my reward, for I have met there some agreeable women (rather too shrieky; but the noise is great) and such men of æsthetic employment as business does not hold in its grip quite till dinner. At the house of an editor who has made so much money with his paper (*The Signal*; its name would say nothing to you; but it has been rather dreadful) that he is now in case to clean up, and who has begun by housing himself,

on the East side, rather too magnificently, I found
some Perennial men, the other day; and there was an
author or two, as authors go in New York, and some
painters who, as things go anywhere, are always more
interesting than authors. We were not without actors,
for it was not a matinée afternoon, and I saw in the
flesh the prevailing actress, though in rather less of
it than I had seen her on the stage. It was pleasant,
or at least piquant; if I were to distinguish so closely
I should say that New York always piques rather than
pleases, and Boston—well Boston at least does not
pique; and it was the more amusing because it was of
that provisional character in which what one may
roughly call celebrity rather than society played the
chief part. The Van der Doeses felt obliged to account for their presence to some of their friends
whom they met, and their friends were likewise
exculpatory; you know what I mean. The celebrity
was nothing to them, or rather worse; I do not care
for it much myself, because it is tiresome; it does
not know what to do with itself; and you do not
know what to do with it; but there were people there
who were all eyes and ears for it. There was a pretty
boy (the boys are so pretty now, with their shaven
faces, which make us eighteen-sixty fellows look so

barbaric with our beards, even when they go no farther than an "educated whisker" or two) who told me afterwards that he was from Iowa, of all places, and teased me with the sense of having seen him before, somewhere. I can't make out yet where it was, if it was really anywhere, but probably it was nowhere. He interested me past the vain quest by asking me when the prevalent actress had turned from me, whether it were she, and then rushed off to a large, flowery young woman—sun-flowery is not too much—and seemed to excite her with the fact as much as himself. Their emotion was so interesting that I did a thing I should not have done when I was under fifty. I followed him up and asked him if he would like to be presented, and the young woman to whom his eager eyes referred me, said, "She would give the world to," and I led them up, and sacrificed them on the shrine of the amiable deity, who had instantly forgotten me, but received us as if we were her oldest friends. After her dispersing welcome, we rather had ourselves on each others' hands, and following an interval in which we treated one another as veteran New Yorkers, we arrived at a sense of our common strangeness, and exchanged our geographical derivations. As the young woman said she had always wanted to see Boston, I could not do less than own that the disappointment of my life was never having seen Iowa. By and by, she asked the young man, who had naturally dropped out of the conversation, if he would not go and hunt up her father, and he presently came back with an old fellow so exactly of my years and of her looks that I had a difficulty in disentangling my consciousness from a tie of kindred. But my contemporary viewed me with an instant of suspicion which I had not experienced from his posterity. He asked, pretty stiffly, if she wanted to go, and she took a fonder leave of me than he. The Van der Doeses turned up in time to break my fall, and they had not quite finished asking me how in the world I had got hold of the Cheese and Churn Trust, when the father returned, with the air of having had it taken out of him by the sunflowery young woman, and said his daughter had been telling him how very kind I had been, and he wanted to thank me. He gave me his card, and when he went the Van der Doeses explained that this was the magnate whose financiering skill is going to embitter our bread to all of us who like butter and cheese with it, and sketched his social career in New York. It could be done briefly, because it had gone no farther than buying a lot worth its width in gold, to build on, and coasting along the shores of society. They added harrowing stories of Western millionaires who had failed to get in, and had gone to Europe to hide their sorrows in the bosom of the aristocracies there; but these Ralsons were inexhaustibly good natured, and the daughter seemed to know how to place the father's money where it would do the most good. She had an instinct or an inspiration concerning the right sort of charities, and if she could find a foothold in Newport, the thing was done. They were very good-natured about it; New York is good-natured about everything; and they were not sorry not to despair of the Ralsons. They did not know who the pretty boy was; perhaps a reminiscence of pre-existence in Iowa (the terms are mine;) or a relation whom Papa Ralson was bringing up to inherit him in the Trust.

I may get very tired of all this. I may go to Europe or I may go to Boston, but if I stay, I shall certainly try to see the Ralsons again.

The excuse of this inordinate letter is that I have not written for so long before; but I will not be so long again. (I seem to be making a play upon words.) At any rate it will last you a day, if it is a day when you cannot go out in your chair. You see

I keep up with your convalescence; for Wally told me something about you, and made it easier for me to break my promise about writing you every week. But I won't do it again—I mean, break my promise.

Yours affectionately,

OTIS.

XII.

From WALLACE ARDITH *to* A. L. WIBBERT, *Wottoma.*
NEW YORK, *January 17, 1902.*

Dear Linc :

I have not written for nearly a week, not because
there was nothing to write, but because there was
and always is only too much. I am one and New
York is three or four millions, and she can beat me
when it comes to a grapple. I want to tell you all
about her, and how she gets me down and rolls me
over, every time I go out of doors, but it is no use
trying; her tricks are too many; she is Hildegunde,
and I happen not to be Siegfried; or not so much
Siegfried as I supposed when I first came here. If I
were wrestling for some other fellow, I might do better, but I am in love with her myself, and more and
more in love every day.

I am now seeing my beloved from the social whirl,
so far as the Ralsons can drag me into the vortex.

Their hospitality continues beyond anything that merit, however modest, could have expected. It is so constant that I find myself getting critical of the cuisine at the Walhondia. In fact, Lamarque's fifty cent table d' hôte is better, in certain touches beyond the reach of art, in certain inspirations. Besides, at Lamarque's the company is always more cultivated than it is at the Walhondia, and on very exceptional Fridays I have got *bouillabaisse* at Lamarque's: the same bouillabaisse that Thackeray made his ballad about; at the Walhondia they never give you bouillabaisse, and I doubt if many of the guests ever heard of Thackeray. But there are worse things than ignorance of literature, and better things than bouillabaisse and I manage to have a good time with the Ralsons at the hotel. I even think that I help them to have a good time, and I don't find myself sorry or ashamed for it. You have to respect a man who has got to the top, and planted himself so squarely there as Ralson has, and America is the best fellow in the world. I take that back, if there is the shadow of slight in it: she is a good, whole-souled girl, and I hope she may get into all the society she wants.

In the meantime she isn't worrying about whether she has reached the real thing or not. The other day

they took me to an afternoon reception—or rather
she did; her father came in later—at the editor of
The Signal's; a kind of housewarming that he was
giving himself in the palace he's just built, and I met
more than four hundred delightful people, whether
they were the four hundred that America is after or
not.   The most delightful of all turned out to be the
charming old fellow whom I talked with in the Park
the day I saw those unmanageable lovers of mine.
The light of recognition faded into perplexity from
the first glance he gave me, and I thought I would
not press upon him the acquaintance which had evi-
dently passed from his lax, senile hold; he proved
even more satisfactory as a nice old Bostonian in
whom I could not feel any menace of rival authorship.   He was as old-school in his afternoon dress,
as he was that day in the Park : very correct, with
not just a New York correctness; but something
more, and something less; it was as if his correctness
were qualified by his intellectuality, which may make
the Boston difference.

He wanted to talk, or to make me talk, of New
York, and was gayly amused at my enthusiasm; he
confessed he did not share it, but professed to be
able to understand it, though I doubt if he did.   I

doubt if he quite grasped me as a product of the roll-
ing prairie, but he did his best, and America seemed
almost to take his mind off New York for a moment.
Miss Everwort, the English actress was there, and he
introduced us.   When she got through with us,
which she did in about half a second, as if we were
so many seats in a house, not to be discriminated, he
stayed chatting with Make and me, till some friends
of his came up; Make told me afterwards they were
the Van der Doeses, which means something supernal
here.   Miss Hally, the chief intervieweress of *The
Signal* bowed to us from a distance, and he asked
very eagerly who she was.   Perhaps you will like to
know, too, and I can tell you what I could not tell
him, that she was much a type as he was.   She is of
a high old Southern family whose passive Unionism
did not keep their fortunes from going down with the
confederates' in the Civil War, and after struggling
along at home, putting up lady-like pickles and pre-
serves for a reluctant market, she came North and
went into journalism.   When Casman took over *The
Signal*, and began to clean it up, he asked her to
join the staff, and that is why she was at his house
the other day.   She goes everywhere in the way of
business, and is welcome to everybody either seeking

or shunning publicity ; for she is an artist and knows when to stop, or when not to begin. The Ralsons know her from her coming to make a story about Mr. R., shortly after their advent here, and they all like her, and help her in the little good turns her left hand does while her right is taking notes for Sunday stories. She got that combination secretary and companion for America and Mrs. Ralson, who has cast already the spell of her personality over the old lady, and the spell of her dictionary over the young one, and though she doesn't like me, promises, I am bound to say, to be a great boon to both of them. I mustn't let you get the notion that I am always on the society heights where you are now beholding me. If I spend my days there from one p. m. to twelve a. m. with the Ralsons, I dwell with the Baysley's from one a. m. till twelve m., in the valley of humiliation, and mostly curse the hour when I was fool enough to come here. They were poor enough before, but just now Baysley has the grippe and they all have their hearts in their mouths for fear he may lose his job if he is kept away from the office long. The old woman and the oldest girl are nursing him, and the youngest is looking after me. I found her waiting to let me in to-night, (or call it this morning,)

for my door key hasn't materialized yet; and when I
said something decent about her father's sickness she
broke down and cried with her head on the table, so
that I wanted to put my arms round her and comfort
her. But I didn't. She is pretty in a pale blonde
way, and you must not put your arms round a girl to
comfort her when she is pretty, and giveth her color
in a pale, blonde way. I suppose she cried a little
more confidentially with me because I got up and
kindled the fire in the range for her this morning—or
yesterday morning, it is now. She has been making
my coffee, and broiling my bacon, since her sister
detailed herself to help her mother look after the old
man; and though she doesn't do them so well as to
make me anxious for either, I did kindle the fire for
her, when I found she wasn't awake at nine o'clock.
You will say that was self-interest, but then you
know I might have gone out and got a breakfast
without smutting my hands. Which would you have
done? I know you will say you would have made
the fire, and I hope you would. It was rather amusing, and rather a touching experience, for it made me
think how I used to kindle the fire for my mother at
Timber Creek, before I went on to be a distinguished
journalist in Wottoma. The poor, sleepy thing came

in after I had got the range red-hot, and wailed out "Oh what did you do it for?" in a way that made the lump come in my throat. I am telling you of these squalid matters a 1:30 a. m., with my dress coat still on, after getting home from the opera with the Ralsons, and gayly parting with Make and her father in their automobile at the door, which this wretched little Essie Baysley let me in at. Life is strange, my dear Linc, but as full of material as an egg is of meat.

Yours ever,

W. Ardith.

XIII.

From Miss Frances Dennam *to* Mrs. Dennam, *Lake Ridge.*

New York, *Jan. 17, 1902.*

Dear Mother :

I have been waiting till I could get warm in my place before writing again, and now I am not only warm, but I seem to be the centre of a life-giving heat for the whole Ralson family. This has its drawbacks. You may think it is easy to sit reading to Mrs. Ralson and cheering her up, and at the same time go out with Miss Ralson in her automobile to those semi-public functions where she needs a chaperon, and I do not need an invitation, only a ticket; but when it comes to the test, it is different. As for Mr. Ralson, I all but sew on his buttons: Miss Ralson seemed disposed, one while, to draw the line at mending his gloves, but she has since withdrawn it.

They are all as good to me as they can be, and if

I could ever love the daughter of a Trust, I should
love Miss Ralson. I have gone back so far on my
principles as to love the wife of a Trust, and she
seems to reciprocate my passion. I have had to hear
so much talk about the "beautiful home" in
Wottoma, from her, that I begin to feel as if I had
come from it, and I have made a picture of it from
memory on the next leaf. You cannot see the
Mississippi from Mrs. Ralson's window, because it is
not in the picture, but you could if you were in the
room there, for the "home" stands on the bluff overlooking the river.

I am not the only pebble on the beach with the
Ralsons, as Miss Ralson would say, or the only sun
in the universe, as *I* should say. There is a young
Wottoma man who comes to see them and seems to
be a general favorite. Miss Ralson says he is "literary," and has been disappointed, not in literature,
but in love; and she is doing what she can to
comfort him, by taking him out to teas, and matinées
and operas, and giving him lunches and dinners here
between times. The old folks are comforting him, too.
Mrs. Ralson almost thinks he helped build the "beautiful home," and he spells me with her when Miss
America takes me out and talks to me about him. I

don't know whether I quite like his taking to comfort so kindly. He is very handsome and very pretty-behaved, but I thing a literary man ought to *lit*, sometimes, and I don't see when Mr. Ardith does, unless it's when he gets home from the opera, and ought to be in bed. He may burn the one o'clock oil, then, but he comes to lunch as blooming the next day as if he had not been sicklied over the least bit. I wouldn't say it to everybody, but you're a mother, or a sister if I include Lizzie, and I'm afraid Mr. Ardith is something of a social self-seeker, and has too good an appetite for the loaves and fishes. I don't really know anything against him, and he's always nice to me, and I'm quite ashamed, but that's the way I feel about him. If you feel differently, don't mind *me!*

The other day Miss Ralson came home from a tea with him, where they had met an old gentleman from Boston who seemed to take both their fancies. It seems that Mr. Ralson had been rather rough with the old Bostonian, and Miss Ralson made him go back and try to make it right, and Mr. Ralson asked him to call, and got a good going-over from his daughter for doing it, which he took as meekly as if he hadn't a cent in the world. But it was not such a mistake after all, and yesterday afternoon Mr.

Binning's card came up, and he after it. Nobody was at home but Miss Ralson and Mr. Ardith, and she sent *him* in to stay with her mother, and brought *me* out. She told him she was not going to have him hanging round, unless she could say he was a cousin, and she couldn't conscientiously say any such thing; and she wanted me because I looked more proper, anyway. This Mr. Binning didn't seem to think I did, but I could see that he didn't know what to make of me, anyway, when she introduced him.

Mother, you're such a purely country person that you won't understand, but my presence said in much better English than I ever use, "Companion, or Secretary, or possibly Typewriter, or Provincial Friend, or Poor Relation, at the best;" and Mr. Binning was all the while trying to fit his behavior to one or the other or all of the possibilities. Every now and then he would say something to me so respectful that I could feel the consideration, and almost the compassion, sticking through, and before I could get off a half-frozen answer, he was switched onto the main-line after Miss Ralson. He had really come to see her, anyway, and I could see that he was perfectly struck up with her gorgeousness. She *is* gorgeous, and makes anybody else in the room look like thirty cents, as she would say ; all the slang you find in my letters is from her. He was very cultivated and talked with her about Europe, and I don't know what else, but especially pictures, I remember. I believe he led up to pictures, and got her to talking of the Titians, so that he could say he must have felt herself quite at home among them. Now, mother, this was where I fell down, (Miss Ralson's expression) for I had to look in a cyclopedia at the Lenox Library to find out that Titian was a painter who mostly painted golden red blondes, and I didn't know till then what Mr. Binning was driving at. But it was pretty when you got it, and Miss Ralson said it was one of the nicest compliments she ever had, when I explained it fully to her this morning. In fact he was as nice as he could be. He is very fine-looking, in an old family portrait way ; we have been trying ever since to make out *how* old a family portrait he is. He is either preternaturally young or prematurely gray, and he is either exquisitely refined or inexpressibly rude. He brought the cards of some ladies of the name of Van der Does, which he framed in the most beautiful apologies for their not calling with him, and begged Miss Ralson's acceptance of an invitation to a tea where there is to be a monologue by a famous monologuist. I shall never know exactly whether he made the invitation include me or not, but if it did it was so delicately done that I might have supposed that it didn't.

It came quite at the end, and when he had gone Miss Ralson stood with the cards in her fingers, twisting them as if she were going to tear them in two, and getting redder and redder, till she was all over the color of her hair, and her blue eyes were like blue fire-works. Then she stopped, and opened her mother's door, and called in, "Come out here, Mr. Ardith," and when he came out she put the whole case to him. He didn't hesitate a moment. "Why, *go*, of course," he said. "It's a semi-public thing, and you needn't more than speak to your hostesses." She ran toward him with her arms open as if she were going to hug him, and shouted out, "You good little worldly angel! You've been six weeks in New York and you know more about it already than I do after a year. But," and this was where she seemed more disappointed than she had been offended before, "I almost wish it had been purely social."

Mother, even the rich have to eat humble pie in New York, I can tell you. I can see that Miss Ralson is going to this function, as they call it, and

I can see that this horrid Mr. Ardith wanted her to go because he saw that she wanted to go, and because he thinks he can get in with the Four Hundred himself. It fairly makes me despise him. She was ready to tear up the cards, if he said so, and fling them in the fire, and he ought to have been man enough to encourage her. She *is* a climber; they came here to get up; but such a fellow as this Mr. Ardith is a creeper and a crawler. Ugh!

Your affectionate daughter,

FRANCES

XIV.

From Mr. Otis Binning *to* Mrs. Walter Binning,
Boston.

New York, *January 19, 1902.*

My Dear Sister:

I am only too glad to respond to your curiosity as I find it framed in the fine doubts, the delicate sniffs, of your yesterday's letter. I do not know that I can add new expression to the physiognimies of my fellow sojourners here, but perhaps I can treat the background so as to throw them into more significant relief.

You ask me whether these Ralson's of mine (you are so good to give them me) are like certain types of the new rich who used to come on from the West to Boston in rather greater force than they do now, to see their sons through Harvard ; and I must indefinitively answer, Not quite. They are Western and they are rich, but the sort of people you instance appeared among us on a semblance of the old duteous terms, which people like the Ralsons frankly ignore. They came among us because they believed, or made believe, that their sons could get through Harvard better with them than without them; and the fact that their presence proved to have nothing to do with the end in view, did not affect the moral elevation of their pretence. But people like the Ralsons come to New York simply because they have got too rich to stay at home, and because they think they can spend their money more agreeably here than where they made it. They come in numbers and variety unknown to our pastoral aforetimes, and without any stay in the St. Louises, the Chicagos, the Cincinnatis, the Pittsburgs, of their native regions. It is said that these provincial centres, which you might think would attract them for a winter or two, have not the social force, or the glamour of the unknown, or the charm of an incomparable grandeur. Boston itself has not this last, and they can come only to New York in the hope of getting their money's worth of whatever they dream of buying here.

In a way their dream is sordid, but they are not always so sordid as their dream, and there is often an ingenuousness in their hope that touches. Some of them come without knowing a soul in the city, but trusting to the fortuities to bring them acquaintance; and they wait upon these with the patience of martyrs and heroes, or, rather, heroines: for it is not the men of their kind who have usually decided the family move on New York. The men might be satisfied to remain at home iu the castles or palaces which they seem always to build in their first opulence, to over-awe the imaginations of their fellow-townsmen; but for their womenkind to be in, if they cannot be of, the metropolis, they leave their local supremacy behind, their great mansions, galleries, greenhouses, libraries of first editions, their whole undisputed state among people who envy if they do not revere them, and come here, and accept seats far below the salt at the second table or the third. They may not always know that they are not sitting in the best places, for there is a great deal of what is apparently society in New York, which is not the real thing, but which satisfies an ignorant aspiration as fully as if it were. The Walhondia for instance, looks like society; the fathers and husbands do not know the difference, and if the wives and daughters find it out, they say nothing about it beyond their family circles. At times, in fact, no one seems more on the outside of society here than another; that is, society itself seems to have no inside. If these new-comers do not find themselves in it, they may think that it is merely a mistake in regard to themselves; that they have been not counted in through accident. Coming here with their ten or twenty millions, they cannot disabuse themselves of the infatuation in which they have lived at home that they are persons of social consequence: they cannot imagine that there are native New Yorkers as rich as they, who are anxious to keep their riches unknown, and would not think it nice to be accepted on account of them; to whom the existence of the vulgar Four Hundred is a matter of supreme indifference; who figure in the society intelligence as little as possible.

But the new-comers are not all, or not altogether bad. My Ralsons are so far from altogether bad that they have a certain wilding charm, and if they can continue sylvanly themselves, they will be the *fine fleur* of the patriciate in a few generations. Their manner does not betray the delusion of so many parvenues that aristocrats are refined people, instead of being people who on coming into their social advant-ages have known how to keep the rude force of their disadvantages; whose cooks, coachmen and lackeys

have, generally speaking, always had better manners,
because they have been obliged to have them. My
Ralson, for instance, is no better behaved now than
he was when he was beginning to make his millions;
he is probably not so well behaved, for then he was
trying by every art, even by his notion of politeness,
to get on; but now his native rudeness has already a
kind of authority, and in his presence I am amused
by a forecast of distinction in him which society will
recognize later. In the meantime he is himself, for
good or bad; he is not afraid to be anything that he
really is. If he is repulsive in his savage sincerity,
he is no more to blame than his daughter, who is
alluring in *her* savage sincerity, and is so much like
him in nature that I am always wondering she is not
like him in character. They are both prodigiously
simple, and their common satisfaction in that pretty
literary youth of mine who is always with them,
greatly commends itself to my fancy. With whatever
dreams of the *jeunesse dorée* the daughter may have
come to New York it would seem as if she had
wakened from them to a delight in him which her
father shares, because he is used to deferring to her
in matters of taste, and perhaps because he secretly
thinks that literature is something the pretty youth

will outlive, when he can be eventually worked into the business; for my Ralson is business, "first, last, and all the time," as he would say, and never so much business as in his abeyance to his daughter.

What the pretty youth thinks of them in his heart, or in that place where the literary soul has its being in the literary man's frequent defect of heart, I do not know. He may not feel their difference from himself, so much as I see it, or he may perceive it as material for future literature. No doubt he is as business in his way as Ralson in his other way. At any rate he has come to New York in obedience to the same law of metropolitan attraction that has drawn the chief of the Cheese and Churn Trust. This law, if it was once operative in Boston is no longer so. I think we *were* once a capital, the capital of New England, but since New England has become more and more lost in the United States, we have ceased to be a capital. We may still be Athens, but we are not the Athens of Socrates, of Pericles; if Athens at all, we are the Athens of the middle or later Empire, whither the young men of generous ambitions resort for culture, but not for the fulfill-ment of their dreams of a literary career. We are no longer the literary, as we are no longer the commercial or the social metropolis, and the young Ardiths of the land (the youth's name is Ardith) would no more think of coming up to us than the old Ralsons.

I am not sure that I have given you the notion of these people which lay so clear in my own mind; I am afraid that I have confused it even there a little; and I am not sure that I can be more convincing about their relation to each other, than about their several psychologies. But I think there can be no cloud in Miss Ralson's mind, whatever vagueness there may be in the pretty boy's; and when she makes it plain that she wants him, neither he nor her father will keep her from having him. It may seem to you a very insufficient outcome of her social aspirations—her father really has none, being purely commercial, though I do not mean by this that outside of his business he is immoral—and yet I cannot help thinking it would be very well. I wish I could make you see it as I do, for I should like you to enjoy with me a genuine New York idyl like this. As a mere witness of the affair, I have all sorts of tender perturbations, hopes, misgivings, desires, and at times, a rich potentiality of unhappiness in it. I am not sure that the youth is so consciously in love as

the maiden, but I have been given to understand
that in things of this kind both sides cannot be
active, and I do not know why the youth should not
be passive, sometimes, instead of the maiden.   It
adds a pleasing poignancy to the situation, and though
the material is not that which I should once have
fancied interesting me, I am now aware of a certain
charm in it which I wish I could impart.   But you,
Margaret, are still in and of Boston, and I am in New
York, liberated to the enjoyment of social spectacles
which you could only view with abhorrence.   If you
tell me you cannot taste my pleasure in the loves of
a young Western journalist and the daughter of one
of the most offensive, and perhaps mischievous of
the modern trusts, I shall not be hurt, but I shall not
press my pleasure upon you.   In fact, I am not sure
that at my age I can altogether justify it to myself.
We will suppose it is a book about some very
commonplace people which I had liked for not very
definable reasons, but which I will not insist upon
lending you unless you urge me.

OTIS.

XV.

From WALLACE ARDITH *to* A. L. WIBBERT, *Wottoma.*

NEW YORK, *Jan. 17, 1902.*

My dear Line:

My letter of the 14th, which has crossed yours, must have given you much of the polite information you seek; but I will try to be a little more specific. The great difference between New York and Wottoma, is quantitative. Most Americans are like most other Americans, whether they have been here two hundred years or twenty, and the New Yorkers have the advantage of the rest principally in being here to the number of two or three millions instead of ten or twelve thousand. Take Wottoma, as a means of comparison. Well, when some high-born dame of yours, say a Daughter of the Black Hawk War, gives an afternoon reception in honor of some weary lecturer on South High Street, most of the ladies come on foot; at the outside you can count up ten or

95

a dozen vehicles at the front gate, including family carryalls, and measly old third-hand hacks from the depot. The men *all* walk, and when they get inside they find the middle-aged and married women packed round the lecturer, trying to catch the well-worn pearls of wisdom that drop from his lips, and the young fellows carrying tea and chocolate from the tables where the young ladies are pouring, and doing their best to flirt a little on the way without spilling the fluids. The girls are willing enough not to be " presented, " and are having as good a time as they can among themselves in circles that it takes all a fellow's courage to break into; and they try to act as if he were intruding when he does, or he feels as if they were. The old fellows hulk round on the outskirts, and keep a good deal on the front porch, and look superior and sarcastic. In all, there are about two or three hundred, and that takes in the whole society of the place.

Well, at this reception of Casman's the other day, there were carriages stretching from his house to the ends of the block both ways, on both sides of the street, and coming and going all the time—all kinds of horse and horseless vehicles, glitteringly new and authoritatively old, with footmen and coachmen on

the boxes, sitting on their overcoats like in the English illustrations, the footman with his hands on his
knees, and the coachman holding the reins in one
hand, and the butt of his whip on his thigh with the
other.   The people were streaming in and out, a
steady current, under a long canopy from the curb-
stone to the door, and the barkers, as they call them,
giving the coachmen their numbers when they came,
and yelling out their numbers when they went.   I
suppose there were four or five thousand men and
women at that reception, but after you got inside the
house was so big that everybody had room.   A
desultory Hungarian band was modestly tucked away
somewhere among the tubs of palms and banks of
flowers, where it could be heard and not seen; and
after you had got your hat and coat check, and joined the ladies of your party, and been inspected by
old Casman and his sister-in-law, and been presented
to his niece, and asked if you had met Miss Everwort,
and told, Well, you must; you sidled off with your
ladies, and looked round to see if you knew any one,
and pretended to be glad you didn't; and talked to
America and her companion as vivaciously as if you
had just been introduced.   Then you asked them if
they were not hungry, and when they owned up, you

found them the way into the dining room, where a lot of men waiters were in charge, and you ordered anything you wanted, and they brought it to you. Everywhere were hundreds of people, looking like half a dozen in the big spaces, and all having the same good time you were. Then you went back to the drawing room to try for a glimpse of Miss Everwort, and if you had our luck with that nice old Bostonian, you were presented to her, and came away feeling that you had had the time of your life, among the five thousand if not the Four Hundred.

Of course, Casman had overdone it a little; he is new to the world though he has been in it about sixty years; but his reception wasn't a bad type; and you were excited by it, and leaned forward in the automobile, and flirted with America so far as to ask for a flower out of her bunch of violets, and tried to smell it, when she gave it to you, under the cold eye of the companion; the old gentleman, after a talking-to America gave him for being rather curt with our nice old Bostonian, seemed to think he would rather walk. Yes, it was all mighty interesting, and I could feel it taking on just the right phrases, at the time. It was the best kind of material, but not socially the finest, though I don't know whether I could make

you understand the difference between that Afternoon, and another Afternoon, which my fine old Boston
cock got us asked to yesterday at the Van der Doeses,
whom he seems to be on familiar terms with.   We
couldn't make out what the occasion was, but the excuse was a monologue by Miss Crawford; and I
wouldn't want a *better* excuse!   It was the most exquisite piece of characterization I could have imagined;
I never saw, or dreamt of seeing, anything like its
perfection; and after it was over, a little well-bred
murmur, and a little tender tapping of finger-tips ran
round the room, and then the host and hostess went
inconspicuously up to the monologuist—the wonderful little genius!—and inaudibly complimented her;
and tea began to come round of itself, somehow.   I
did not know but America had made a break with
that laugh of hers, but I guess not.   The note of those
people seemed to be doing what they pleased, if they
had known what; and I suppose they would have
laughed if they had felt like it; but if it wont appear
invidious to such an aristocrat as you, I will say that
they hardly seemed up to the art of the thing as the
people at Casman's would.   Our old Bostonian was,
though, and he asked America if she would like to
speak to Miss Crawford, and he got Mrs. Van der Does

to introduce her; and America took both her hands
into hers, and I looked away for fear she was going
to kiss her.

Now, what I mean by the quantitative difference
between New York and other places, is that these
two sorts of things keep going on here all the time,
the Casman sort and the Van der Does sort, on a scale
that you simply can't imagine in Wottoma. *You*
can have the Casman sort once in a winter, but of
course not the Casman size, when the right lecturer
comes along to make it with; and you have got the
root of the Van der Does sort in the first settlers,
which will break out a hundred years from now,
maybe, like a century plant, but here the century
plant blooms every day. Understand? No, you wont,
you can't! You will have to come here and see for
yourself; and that makes me want to tell you something. Don't give it away, especially in print, till
I've tried my hand; but old Casman sent for me the
morning after his reception, and asked me how I
would like to do something for the Sunday *Signal*.
I guess Miss Hally had been putting up a job on him,
and he had got the idea that I could write, say, "The
Impressions of a Provincial," giving a simple, frank
account of New York, from a fresh country arrival's

point of view, that would sweep "this fair land of ours" from ocean to ocean. I took to the notion, at once, and I am going to make the effort. It will give me a chance to work in the material that has been piling up on my hands since I came, and I believe I can do something that will plant me at the feet, at least, of George Ade, if I can get the right attitude; I'm going to invent a character for my provincial. And then, Linc, don't you see? If I'm ever in the saddle, here, I am going to pull you up behind. If New York can't carry double, I am very much mistaken.

The grippe still hangs on with poor old Baysley, but we manage to rub along, somehow; the old lady and Jenny have got it, but they are light cases. I still make the fires for Essie, though I feel as if I were kindling them with the budding laurels from my own brow.

Always yours, Linc.

W .A.

XVI.

THE WALHONDIA, *January the nineteenth, Nineteen
hundred and two.*

My dear Caroline :

I am so glad you think you can come, and I will
try to make a date for you—the earlier the better. I
would have written sooner to say so, but I have had
more on my hands than usual, as you will see by this
being in typewriting. I will have to talk it over
with father, and see what his engagements are.
March is not a very good month, on account of
being nearly all Lent, this year, but if you do not
mind having rather a quiet time, it will be all right.

Thank you for the *hint.* I supposed it was off
for good, but I see no reason why you should not
try to have it on again, if you wish. There has
been no allusion to the matter, since the first time,

102

and I don't know just how the land lies. I should *say* that your engagement had been accepted as final, and that the announcement to the contrary had better not come through me. If you prefer, you can let things rest, till you come on, and then you can look the ground over for yourself. I don't see how there can be any objection to a girl's changing her mind once or twice if she wants to.

Do let me hear from you soon again, and if you are still decided to come in March, I have no doubt that I can arrange for your visit then as well as later. The great thing is to have you here.

Yours affectionately,

AMERICA RALSON.

XVII.

From W. Ardith *to* A. L. Wibbert, *Wottoma.*

NEW YORK, *Jan'y, 19, 1902.*

Dear Linc:

This afternoon when I got home from a matinée
with America Ralson and Miss Dennam, I found the
Baysley family very much cheered up. The old
gentleman had taken a decided turn for the better,
and Jenny and the old lady were able to be about,
helping Essie get the "tea" which I knew was to be
their evening banquet. My heart smote me when I
thought of the dinner I was going down to have at
Lamarque's, and I would have been glad to ask the
whole family to join me there; but that was not prac-
ticable, and so I compromised on Essie. "What is
the reason you can't go with me to Lamarque's *this*
evening?" I said, as if we had talked before of her
going with me sometime, though we never had; and
the joyful color flushed up in her face and faded out,

and she answered with another question, "What do you mean?" In answer I merely added, "Then we could take in a vaudeville show, and still get home early." "I couldn't leave," she said, and she put the plate she was holding softly down on the table, as if it were her last hope, and sighed so pathetically that I saw I must carry the thing through. "You might ask," I suggested. "Or no, *I* will," and I called into the kitchen from the dining-room where we were, "Mrs. Baysley, Essie says she won't go with me to dinner at Lamarque's, and to Keith's afterwards. Can't you make her?" "Oh, you awful"— Essie began, catching her breath, but the joke was so prodigious that none of them were proof against it. When her mother made sure that I was joking in earnest—the Baysley's think I am a tremendous joker—she said, "Why, of course Essie must;" and then Jenny began to offer Essie her best clothes; and between refusals and protests, and laughs and outcries from the women, and feeble crows of command from the old man in his room, Essie was forced to drop everything, and do as I bid.

They did get her very tastefully together, and in such good time that when she came to me in the parlor, with her mother and sister following limply but proudly after her, I was disposed to linger over her sympathetically as long as they liked. It is astonishing how soon women take on New York in their dress when they come here. Mrs. Baysley told me that these were just the girls' old Timber Creek things; they had been too busy since they came to get anything for anybody. But it was Timber Creek with the difference that comes from studying the fashions on the streets and in the shop windows here.

Essie is too little to look distinguished, but no one is too little to be *chic*, and *chic* was what the eyes at Lamarque's said of her when she showed like a pretty flower through the rifts of the cigarette smoke: the smoking goes on straight through the dinner at Lamarque's. Those cub authors were out in force at their corner table, and between their talk about themselves and each other, I knew from the way they stared at us that we were giving them a topic. Every fellow there was making mental note of us, and heaven knows how many poems, sketches, studies and stories Essie went into on the spot. I laughed inside to think how I had got the start of them all, and how none of them saw us more objectively than I did, or felt our quality as material half as intelligently. I tried to make Essie understand who they

were, and appreciate their greatness; but she was
unconscious as a child through everything. Of
course a child is not unconscious of its looks or its
behavior, and I knew that she knew she was pretty
and was anxious to be very correct. She peered
round to see whether she should take her hat off, and
then kept it on, as if she had dined at Lamarque's all
her life. The lady at the next table had her gloves
on the table, and after the soup came I saw Essie's
gloves under the edge of her plate. The *garçon*—
he knows me and my French and flattered me and it
with a smiling "Bonsoir, monsieur," that made
Essie's blue eyes dance—asked whether I would
have red wine or white, and when it came white, as I
had ordered, I offered to pour it into Essie's glass,
and I saw her tremble as she gasped out, "Oh, do you
think I'd better?" I said, "Well, it isn't very good,"
and I put the cork back into the bottle for both of
us, and I could feel her heart lighten of the misgivings that the wine had burdened it with. She began
to be innocently gay, and to let out that she had
noticed everything, and taken in that we were dining
in the front parlor of what had been a private house,
and that the other dining-room was the back parlor,
and the wall-paper had not been changed since the

family had left the place. She kept down her surprise at the alertness with which we were served, and she took Lamarque's personal intervention, in the matter of crowding in a table for new-comers where there was already scarcely room to turn around, as things of a life-long experience, and she helped me receive with dignity the old fellow's compliment when he visited us to hope that we found everything right. At first she was not going to speak of the food, but I spoke of it and then she was very glad to be allowed by politeness to praise its variety and novelty. I knew she had never seen a dinner in courses before, but she went through it as if it were her habit, keeping an eye on me to see what I liked or left, and following suit. I could see she was anxious not to disgrace me, in any way, and I made it easy for her now and then to pass a dish that she did not want, by saying that I never cared much for that dish. It was not a *bouillabaisse* night, and I pretended to be very sorry for that; but it was an ice-cream night, and I could see that when the small flat block of chocolate and vanilla came, Essie was without a regret. Over the little cups of coffee she began to betray that she had been noticing the company, and she gave an excellent imitation of

being supremely interested in my favorites: the old
Spaniard, or old Italian, who always gets half way
through his dinner at a small corner table before he
is joined by a deeply hatted lady and her husband
coming freshly in from the cold outside, and pressing
about the grate at their backs till they forget it in
their criticism of the dishes; the prematurely gray-
haired and eye-glassed lady whom I call my Mystery,
and who eats all through her dinner with a book
propped open against a tumbler; the middle-aged
French mother with her daughter still in short skirts
and very *jeune fille*, whom she lets see nothing except
out of the corners of her eyes, but gives half a bottle
of Lamarque's California claret, while the girl sits
demure, and does not speak even when Lamarque
comes up to compliment her mother in their native
tongue.

I looked at my watch at last, and said, If we expected to get in many of those stunts at Keith's!
and Essie started nervously, and then controlled herself and let old Lamarque help her on with her jacket
(he likes to help the ladies on with their jackets) as
unconsciously as if she were used to it every night.
She bowed silently to his "Bon soir, madame!" and
went out before me so gracefully, so prettily, that

happening to look back over my shoulder at the cub
authors' table, I saw them all staring their admira-
tion, and one fellow bowed involuntarily. "Do they
know you?" she asked, and then I reflected that a
girl always has eyes in the back of her head, and
need not seem to be turning round to see what con-
cerns her. I mumbled something about its being the
custom for people to bow at Lamarque's to the parting guests; but I was easily more rattled than she
was.

In fact, her ignorance of the world that she has
been living on the edge of for the last six months
is so untroubled that everything but the innocent joy
of our night's adventure was lost upon her. She is
scarcely more than a child in years, and she is still a
child in nature, so that I could give her this pleasure
as safely as if she were ten years old; and I decided
not to do it by halves. The gorgeous old fellow in
livery who stands before Keith's and owns up when
you put him on his honor, said there was not a seat
left in the house, and her face fell; but I asked cool-
ly, "What is the matter with a couple of box-seats?"
and he confessed that there might be some box-seats;
I could try inside. So I blew in two extra half
dollars, and before Essie knew it we were in the stage-

box rapt in the monologue of the Man in the Green
Gloves.

I won't go through the whole list of standard
stunts: the girl with the Southern accent that sings
pathetic ballads of the lost cause, and then coon songs
for her recalls; the tramp-magician that praises and
blames himself with "Oh, pretty good! oh, pretty
rotten!" the tremendously fashionable comedy sketch,
all butlers and footmen, and criss-cross love-making
between Jack and some one else's wife so as to cure
Jack's wife of making love with the other lady's
husband and convince her that there is nobody like
Jack; the Viennese dancers, and the German acro-
bats and acrobatesses; the colored monologuist, and
the man in a high hat and long overcoat, unbuttoned
to show his evening dress, who balances feathers on
the point of his nose and keeps a paper wad, an open
umbrella and a small dinner bell tossing in the air:
they were all there and more too, and nothing that
any of them said or did was lost upon Essie Baysley.
I could see her storing it up for the family's joy at
second hand; and she did not give herself away by
any silly outcries or comments. She bore herself like
a lady; if not like a real lady, then like an ideal lady;
she watched the stage with one eye, and me with the

other, and after she had taken a modest fill of these
pleasures, she asked me the time, and said she ought
to be going, for she did not want to leave them alone
very long.

She meant the other Baysleys, and would not let
me stop for ice-cream on the way home, and then
was penitent and apologetic for not thinking I might
have wanted it very much.   As a study she was
charming, but in and for herself, a little of little Essie
I found went a long way; and an evening of her conversation did not end prematurely at half past ten.
I delivered her over intact to her mother and sister,
waiting up for us, without so much as claiming at the
foot of the stairs the kiss that Timber Creek usage
would have entitled me to.   In fact I forced down
the ghost of a silly apprehension about myself and
the child which I had felt, off and on, ever since she
broke down and cried that night when I condoled
with her about her father's sickness, and the trouble
they were all in.   I had given her the time of her
life, and heaven had kept me from saying or doing
anything to mar it.   I had done the whole hapless
family the greatest pleasure that they had had since
they came to New York, and made them feel, as the
old man, wakeful with the rest, croaked out from his

sick room, like they were back in Timber Creek again. Their gratitude cost me just $3.50, counting in carfares and the fee to the waiter at Lamarque's, and I call that cheap. I don't exactly see how the experience will work into the "Impressions of a Provincial," unless as an episode of Bohemia, or something of the sort, but it is pure literature as it lies in my mind, and I lend it to you, my dear Lincoln, for your exclusive enjoyment till I can get a scheme that will carry it to the public.

Yours ever,

W. A.

I find a note here from the glorious America, reminding me of my promise (I never made any !) for the opera Monday night. I am to dine at their hotel first, she tells me.

XVIII.

From MISS FRANCES DENNAM *to* MRS. DENNAM, *Lake Ridge, N. Y.*

NEW YORK, *Jan. 19, 1902.*

Dear Mother :

This has been "my busy day" with Miss Ralson, and Mrs. Ralson has not been in it for a moment. It has lasted for a good while, and I have just now got home after dining at the hotel, and talking over with Miss Ralson the matinée we were at this afternoon. That is, I talked of the matinée, and she talked of Mr. Ardith, who went with us. He came on here, you know, in December to put his broken heart together; and now it seems that the girl who broke it is sorry she did it. At any rate she has disengaged herself from the man that she jilted him for, and is feeling round to see how she can get Mr. Ardith back. This is the short of it, but the long of it is much more exciting, and I wish I could give it

114

to you. As Miss Ralson says, it would make a book, and I am not writing a book. I am not sure that I ought to be writing this letter, but I know that you will be as silent as the grave, and so I will keep on.

The joke is that before Miss Ralson knew anything about the disengagement she had asked the girl here to visit her; they are old friends, and she was very cordial, but to-day I have written a letter for her, taking back a good deal of the cordiality, and a little of the invitation; and if you can't guess why, you are not the mother I took you for. Mr. Ardith seems to have been here, day in and day out, ever since he came to New York, and he has not had to *push in.* There! I will say that much, and I am ashamed of saying anything. If I add that there is no accounting for tastes, and that if Mr. Ardith was the Last Man, I would take my chance with the next, you can understand how I feel about it. Of course I keep a straight face, and when Miss Ralson takes ground so high that no personal feeling can be supposed to be up there with her, I don't do anything to let her dream that I am *on,* as she would say. It is no business of mine if she wants to throw herself away; only if she does I suppose I shall be out of a job.

And I had begun to like the job, so much! Yes mother, your bad little girl finds life in the Walhondia very, very comfortable, and if there were no money in the job still it is so comfortable that she could not bear to have it stop. Besides, I do like the Ralsons, the whole family, and I don't know but my affections would go round the whole Trust. They are good people; even the wicked father is good in his way; and as for the mother, well, I won't say you haven't some cause to be jealous. She depends upon me so much that perhaps she would want me to keep on here, after her daughter left off; but I'm afraid I should be so heartbroken I couldn't stay.

I got my envelope, as the wage-earners say, this evening, and I enclose the pleasing contents to you. I don't suppose you will want to anticipate the interest, and I certainly don't want to give old Grottel any agreeable surprises. But my first earnings were news too good to keep. They may be my last, so be careful of them. If Miss Ralson asked me my honest opinion of Mr. Ardith, aud pressed me to give it, I am afraid I should, and that would settle *me*. With love to Lizzie,

Your affectionate daughter,

FRANCES.

XIX.

From WALLACE ARDITH *to* A. LINCOLN WIBBERT,
Wottoma.

NEW YORK, *Jan'y 20, 1902.*

My dear Linc:

I wish, while it is fresh in my mind, that I could give you a notion of my whole evening, as a pendant for you to hang on memory's wall with the picture of Bohemian life which I painted for you in my last. This has in fact been another episode of Bohemian life as far as I'm concerned, and in a kind of way—a more expensive way—the Ralsons are gypsying here, too. Perhaps even our ancient Boston friend has broken bounds in our company, and is secretly outlawed along with us; though as far as looks go we were all as absolutely conventional as any party in the boxes of the opera to-night.

Apparently the party was made for him, and I was asked to meet him at dinner, either from the social poverty of the Ralsons, or because I am social riches, which they chose to lavish on him with the gilt-edge victuals and drink. I leave you to decide the question, as old Ralson himself would. He was rather pressed into the service of America, and he did not go beyond looking the part of indulgent father, and munificent host. He had one of the best tables, especially decorated for the occasion, with the costliest floral exhibit that money could buy, and served by several of the handsomest and most exorbitant slaves, under the eye of their chief who kept it vigilantly out for them from any quarter where he happened to be. In that vast, indiscriminate splendor, Ralson had bought himself as much personal attention as he could have got at Larmarque's for fifty cents; but having achieved the distinction, he rested in his dignity of host, and let his daughter manage the talk. I must say, he looked the part of an old barbaric aristocrat to perfection, with his long white mustache sweeping across his face, and his white hair snowily drifted on his head. I hope I am not indiscreet in saying that America's shoulders dismayed me with their marble mass; I ought to be used to them by this time, but to-night they seemed to me a fresh revelation of her beauty.

I will not specify my own share in the *ensemble*, but together I think we gave an imitation of people who had always been in the habit of dining in that state and going to the opera afterwards, which ought to have imposed upon even such an old worldling as Mr. Binning. I do not know how far he divined us; in the talk between him and Mr. Ralson which I caught, I heard him gently offering the old fellow opportunities of self-interpretation which I do not believe were all wasted. They even left him exhausted in one sense if not another, and America promptly rescued Mr. Binning from his silence, and turned him over to me, with a trust in my ability to take care of him in conversation which I hope was not mistaken. I would rather have talked with her, to be honest, but I was not going back on her.

I believe the old fellow enjoyed every moment of it, but for us it was work; and it was work between the acts at the opera, where we renewed the struggle with fresh vigor. There is no use pretending, my dear Lincoln, that there is any common ground except mortality between youthfulness and elderliness; they can be a little curious about each other, but not interested after that little curiosity is satisfied. The best time of our evening was once when Mr. Binning went out to call on some friends of his in one of the boxes, and Mr. Ralson went out, as he did at the end of every act for something to support him through the next. Then America became suddenly psychological, and asked me what I thought all that display was like. She meant the necks and arms and dresses and jewels, and the black and blond heads, and the blur of faces, which the opera glass distinguishes and the eye leaves in a shining nebulosity. Of course I said, " Like a terraced garden of flowers, " but she answered, " No, like a glorified confectioner's, " ; and I had to own that with the weak, pale tones of the house decorations and the electric lights accenting the prevailing pinks and whites, and the golden and glassy surfaces of the women, and all the sharp variations of light colors, it was of the effect of candy. Then she rather astonished me by bursting out: " Huylers, Huylers! chocolates, and peppermint candies, and ice-cream sodas! And I am getting sick of it all! Those people seem to be willing to live on sweets, but I should like a few morsels of plain humanity, shouldn't you?" I suggested that those would be cannibalism for me; and she said "Oh, pshaw! you know what I mean, " and without any act of transition, she said she would like to know what I really thought of her, anyway. I ventured to say, "Everything!" and that made her laugh, but sadly; and she said she hoped no friend of hers supposed she cared for the kind of life she had been leading, or trying to lead. Then again she leaped the chasm and demanded to know how I would like to be like Mr. Binning, at his age; she supposed he was intellectual, too. "If I could write poetry," she zigzagged on, "I should write a poem about such a thing as this, where everybody is playing a part, as much off the stage as on it, and try to show what each one really was thinking, all the time. "A sort of masque," I suggested, and she said, "I don't know what a masque is," and just then Mr. Binning came back, and began to make his neat, apt remarks about the opera. It was *Tristan und Isolde*, and he said he was of the age of Italian opera himself, and a thing like this made him feel as if he had outlived his youth, "Which people wouldn't suspect, otherwise," he concluded.

He seemed to have felt the hardship of having his flow of soul dammed up in him where he had been. But I wished he had stayed away longer, for that revelation of America was precious. There was a little more of it when we had dropped Mr. Binning at his hotel after the opera, and I could see her kick her revered father on the shin with her slipper; Mr. Binning's going had left us both on the seat in front of her. "Don't you wish you were back in Wottoma, old gentleman?" she asked, and when he grunted that New York was good enough for him, she said, "Well, *I* do." She rather snubbed me when I offered some excuses for the metropolis, and said, "Oh, yes, it's all copy for you." (She has got the word from me, I suppose.) At the hotel she jumped out and ran over the carpeted pavement toward the door, as if she were not going to bid me good-night, and then she whirled round, and caught my hand in her large clasp. "Are you coming to lunch to-morrow—with Miss Dennam?" I answered mechanically, I supposed so, and she said, "Well, see that you do," and wrung my hand, and ran on again, while her father smiled under one side of his mustache, and winked a sleepy eye at me.

As I understand it, what this wink expressed was nothing personal to me, but only something to the effect that America was doing exactly what she pleased; it recognized that she always had done so, and could be trusted always to do so, and still to do the right thing. It gave me the sense of a sublime faith in her on his part, which was to the credit of both, and it made me like the old fellow better than I have. I don't know that I have disliked anything but his money, or rather the way he got it; but even that looks less baleful in the light of his wholesale love for such a wholesouled girl. There is growth in that girl; she can think as well as feel, and I begin to respect her mind as well as her nature, which is laid out on the largest scale. You are not to imagine that there is anything but the most dispassionate appreciation in this. I have had my medicine, and I am cured.

Yours ever,

W. ARDITH.

XX.

New York, *Jan. 21, 1902.*

My Dear Sister :   ·

Your letter found itself punctually at the Perennial, this morning, when less punctually I found myself at my nine o'clock breakfast there. It added the fragrant aroma of your spirit to that of my coffee, and the joint stimulus ought to be sufficient for the pleasing task of answering it as instantly as you require. But if, at this pleasant window overlooking two miles of woodland in the Park, I fail of the responsive inspiration, blame not me, but the hospitalities of my Ralsons, which began last night with dinner, and ended with opera. As you hardly deny and disclaim any interest in my generalizations concerning their kind, and desire only my personalizations concerning them, and more specifically her, you will

124

perhaps forgive them for getting so promptly into the excuses with which every letter ought to open.

As nearly as I can understand, the affair was made for me, in recognition of some civilities of mine, and if they added my young friend from Iowa—I forget whether I have ever said his name was Ardith—it was no more from Miss Ralson's wish to have him for herself than from her desire to save her father and me from each other. The mysterious Mrs. Ralson is so invalided as never to appear within my social ken, and the Trust himself is not of a conversation that holds out long in my quarter. He early decided that I was intellectual, I think, and with the admirable frankness of his class, he conceived of me—no doubt in a delicate compliment to your sex,—as a kind of mental and moral woman, to whom a real man, a business man, could have nothing to say after the primary politenesses. I do not know why he should rank me below Mr. Ardith, as I feel he does, unless it is because Mr. Ardith is still young enough to be finally saved from intellectuality, and subsequently dedicated to commerciality. But in the meantime he seems to have agreed with his daughter that the interposition of this nice boy's mental substance was our only hope against wearing upon each other. The boy himself seemed to have the same inspiration, and Miss Ralson and he rent their souls asunder, from time to time, and filled the precarious space between the Trust and me when the friction of our reciprocal silences became too apparent.

They did not know it, but I fancy, my dear Margaret, that these sacrifices bored them. It was worse at the opera than at the dinner even, for the Trust went out at the end of each act and did not come back till the curtain had risen on the next; so that though it does not much amuse me to call on people in their boxes, I left those poor young things to themselves as often as I could. I would much rather have stayed and talked with them, but beside the congenital difficulty that youth has in orienting itself with age (or middle age, if you civilly insist) and getting all sorts of hindering scruples and respects that intercept the common view, out of the way, they were drawn exclusively together by the passion whose charming play I was so loath to miss the least of. It is in that exquisite moment when alone such a thing can interest a third person: it had not yet owned itself to either, I fancy; when both have owned it, then the blow is given; it might as well be marriage, and done with it.

That it is coming to that, with whatever fond de-
lays and wanderings, I have no doubt, and that it is
arriving more rapidly with her than with him is quite
as certain.   That is what forms for me its peculiar
fascination, which is also a poignant regret that you
are not here to share it with me at first hand.   These
young people are really worthy of your observance,
Margaret; for though they are not, by the widest
stretch of charity, to be accounted of that Boston
cousinship which nature has made so large as to include nearly every type of merit, still they have a
wilding beauty of being, at least in this supreme moment, which I think you would feel beyond any one
else.   You have the poetic imagination to which the
girl's greater courage of her emotions would justify
itself; and when you saw her " eyes of sumptuous
expectation," fixed on him, as if in the brute phrase,
she could eat him, your generous instinct would find
the anthropophagy divine.

As for the youth, I am sure he would at least not
be sorry to be eaten.   Yes, I am sure of that; or else
I am sure that in his place I should not.   It was delightful, when I came back just before the last act,
to see them struggle away from their interest in each
other, and turn to me with the topic it had masked

itself in. "We were talking," she promptly began, "about the play off the stage here," and he turned to me as if he were intensely anxious for my wisdom. "Have you ever noticed the programme?" and she gave me her play bill, opened to that monumental leaf on which the names of the box-owners, and the nights when they appear, are inscribed. "Do you think that is good taste?"

Then I began to take a Polonius part in another play, more subjective than the make-believe of the boxes, and entered upon a disquisition of American civilization, of which that leaf seemed to me one of the most signal expressions. I said that we were the frankest people in the world in recognizing the thing that was, and that when our democracy found itself in the possession of an aristocracy, with coronets and tiaras and diadems of precious stones, it wished to feel the fact in its bones. It was not the nobility in the boxes who wanted that list printed; they existed but for each other alone; and it was the commonalty in the parquet and uppermost galleries who enviously exulted in it. I added that of course it was droll, and that in the presence of the old American ideal it might make one's flesh creep; but that the old American ideal was nowadays principally appreciable by its absence; and how, after all, did that leaf essentially differ from the repetitions of the society intelligence in all the papers?

The young people followed me with an ostensible constancy; they applauded the best points; I believe Mr. Ardith felt a literary quality in what I was saying; but she was hearing *him* in it all, and in the end my discourse was a solution of themselves, in which they were both chiefly conscious of each other. It amused me, but at last saddened me, and when I got home to bed, I reflected long upon the case. It was so old, that love business, and though it had the conceit of an eternal novelty in its dim antiquity and did freshen itself up in the perpetually changing conditions, it was really the most decrepit of the human interests.

I expect you to deny this, and in making you a present of my evening's experience, I promise not to take it hard of you if you say it is perfectly charming, and altogether different from the stale rubbish in the novels you have been reading.

OTIS.

XXI.

From Miss Frances Dennam *to* Mrs. Dennam,
Lake Ridge.

New York, *Jan'y 21, 1902.*

Dear Folks:

I include Lizzie in the address because I know that she will enjoy this letter as much as you, mother, and because she ought to share fully in the guilt of it, if it is wrong to write it. I don't know as it's betraying a *confidence*, exactly, for there was nothing less confided, as I understand such things. But anyway, I am tempted beyond my strength, and here goes !

Miss Ralson certainly is funnier than a goat. She had Mr. Ardith here to-day again lunching, as usual; she has got to telling him it is to meet *me ;* and after it was over, and he was gone, she began on him, almost as soon as his back was turned. I must try to give you what she said in her own words, for they are half the fun. She said, "Now, Miss

Dennam, I really did make this lunch to have Mr. Ardith meet you; for I wanted you to look him carefully over, and tell me just what you think of him. You needn't ask why, but when you have given me your candid opinion, I will tell you why. I don't promise to be ruled by your opinion, so you needn't be afraid to speak up, for you wont be held responsible. Begin! Do you think he's handsome?"

Her way of talking helped me put my back up, and I answered as plumply as she asked, "He isn't my style of beauty, but I do think he's handsome. I like a larger man; and I'm so old-fashioned that I prefer a man with a beard, or a mustache, at least, instead of clean-shaved. I think your father must have been a very handsome man," and I didn't say this to flatter her, and she knew it. " Father was very well in his day, but the style is different, now, and Mr. Ardith is more in the style. Do you think he's good?" " I don't know what he's done!" "Goodness is being as well as doing, and you needn't try to slip out of it *that* way. Do you think he's selfish?" " Yes, I do. I think all the men I've ever seen are selfish, except my father." " Well, that's so, and I don't suppose some people would let me except *my* father, though *I* know he's the best father in the world. Yes, I suppose Mr. Ardith may be called selfish. "

She looked a little down, and I had to say, " I shouldn't call him selfish so much as self-centered. He's so wrapped up in what he's doing, or going to do, that he can't think of anybody else. He never does nice little polite, thoughtful things like Mr. Binning, for instance. The woman that married Mr. Ardith "—
" It hasn't come to that point in the conversation yet, " she broke in, and I had to laugh; she kept her face straight. " But I see what you mean. She would have to go way back and sit down when he wanted to work. Well, go on ! " She put up her hands and clasped them behind her neck, the way her father does, and she slid down in her chair like him, and— if I *must* say it—stretched her legs out before her, as he does his, when he is feeling just right; and I suppose she will be his figure at his age. " Do you think he's in love ? " " No, I don't. With Miss Deschenes, you mean ? " She sat up. " *With Miss Deschenes !* He *never* was in love with that conceited, cold-hearted, lean, black little— Or, if he ever was, he's good and over it long ago. I mean with *me !* "

Well, mother—and Lizzie—that did rather take my breath, used as I am to her frankness; but I was not going to be scared into saying anything I did not think, and I said, " I think he's in love with himself. " I decided that this was noncommittal enough, but it did not daunt Miss Ralson. She laughed and said, " Well, so am I, and I don't wonder at him a bit. He'll be in love with me fast enough, when I say the word ; and I've only been waiting to be sure that I'm in love with him. And now I *am* sure. I wanted to hug him, he's so dear, all through the opera last night, but I didn't because I hated to scandalize him ; and to-day when he went away it was all I could do to keep from saying, ' Take me with you, precious, and don't remember to bring me back ! ' He's good, if he *is* selfish ; and he's pure, and he's got more sense, and more wit, and more soul, and more intellect ! And if he wants to, he is going to be the greatest writer that ever lived ; and he shall, too, for all me. I would rather slave for him, scrub, cook, take in washing, and do plain sewing, than be Queen of the Four Hundred. The Four Hundred ! What do I care for the Four Hundred ? That dream is past, thank goodness, and it was *he* that come to wake me from the worst nightmare *I* ever had. We can go abroad—I know father will let us—and you can stay with mother ; or go back to Wottoma with

her; and we can settle down in some quiet place,
like Rome, or London—and he can write his head
off. My, but it'll be great!" She jumped up, and
caught me round the neck, and kissed me; and I
could hardly get away. "You think I ought to be
ashamed, but I'm not. What is there to be ashamed
of? I shouldn't be ashamed, now, if he didn't have
me; but he will. And I'll get Caroline Deschenes
to come on, and when I've got her here I'll spring
it on her that she is to be one of the bridesmaids,
and you've got to be the other. We'll have the
greatest *time!*"

She smothered her face in my neck, and ran out
of the room, and left me there not knowing what
to think. I don't know yet, and I wish you and
Lizzie would take the job off my hands. I knew
well enough what I *ought* to think; but when I remember how she has always been allowed to have
and do all she pleased, and how, after all, she is
so generous and big-hearted with everyone and not
the least spoiled, I am not able to think what I
ought. It isn't exactly *usual* for a girl to talk out
her feelings so; but if the feelings are right in
themselves what harm is there in talking them out?
That is what I ask myself, and then I say that if

anyone is to blame it is I for telling you this, and you for letting me, and so we had better be pretty modest.

Your affectionate daughter and sister,

FRANCES.

For pity's sake don't let Lizzie suppose I want *her* to take after Miss Ralson! She hasn't got the money, for one thing.

XXII.

From WALLACE ARDITH *to* A. L. WIBBERT, *Wattoma.*

NEW YORK, *Jan. 23, 1902.*

My Dear Lincoln:

I address you in this serious way not because I have got anything against you, but because I have got something against myself. I am to blame, for I put myself in the way of it when I might have seen it coming; but I can swear that I meant to do nothing to make it come. If I thought of it at all, I thought it would be a bore, but I never supposed it would be a tragedy. Of course, I was all kinds of an ass to come here, but I can bear myself witness that I did it from the kindest motive in the world, though it wasn't any the less assinine on that account. I had a good deal better jumped at the poor old woman and swept her off the earth when she hinted at my coming.

Well, the grippe has begun to let up on the old man, so as to get a new hold of the old woman and Jenny, and if it had chosen either little Essie or me, it would have been better for us; I could have advised it what to do, if it had consulted me, but it didn't. I have not only been kindling fires, and helping Essie with the housework generally, between the times of scrapping with the Ralsons on the ragged edge of the Four Hundred, but I have been taking my turn nursing old Baysley. I don't know what I shall do now, with Jenny and her mother sick, except cook all the meals and lend Essie a hand with the wash; she isn't much of a cook, or laundress either. I suppose it reads comically, but it doesn't *live* so, and if you will add the fact that I have had to intercede personally with Mr. Ralson for old Baysley, you will have the touch of pathos that is always supposed to give the humorous such fine relief.

There has been pathos enough in it, ever since I knew that the old man here was in the employment of the Cheese and Churn Trust, and that he had found out I was a friend of the Ralsons, and believed that if I wanted to I could do something in the way of promotions and appropriations. I don't say that I have seen this in either of the girls, or at least not in Essie, but I've divined it in the old people; they couldn't have been more deferential if I had been Ralson in person. When Baysley began to get over the grippe so far as to be more anxious about living than dying, he couldn't keep himself from asking me to "use my influence." Imagine what a dose that was!

The Ralsons had brought me home here in their automobile several times, but I hadn't found it essential to tell them who my landlord was, and now I would have to come out with it, when it would have the effect of something I had been hiding. Baysley was afraid of losing his job, and of course I couldn't say no; I put the case to Mr. Ralson, last night, in the presence of America, and I had him whipped as badly as I was. We were at the play, and it was between the acts of Mrs. Pat Campbell's "Second Mrs. Tanqueray," when we were all rather broken up.

The old gentleman had forgotten about Baysley, whom he had sent on here I guess because he was not much use anywhere else, and I don't believe he would have hesitated even if he had been alone with me. But it was all I could do to keep America from leaving the play and driving right up here with a hamper full of Christmas goods, like the good angels

in those old Dickens stories. She got the facts of
the family sickness out of me in about a minute, and
when she found that the girls were not pretty, to
speak of, and the youngest was doing the work herself (I suppressed my share) she wanted to fill the flat
with trained nurses and professed cooks. After the
play was over, and they brought me here her father
had to use force to keep her from coming up-stairs
with me to see how they were getting along; and
nothing would do but to let her come here this
morning. I don't know how early she will come, but
perhaps Nature may assist Art, and she will oversleep
herself, though I am taking no chances, and am writing this letter between kindling the fire in the kitchen
and calling the miserable Essie to get breakfast.

"And is that all?" I fancy you asking. I wish it
were!

When I came home last night, the old man was
waiting up along with the little girl, and he was so
anxious that even when I shouted at him, "It's all
right, Mr. Baysley," he couldn't take it in. Essie
had to say it over to him, and then he flopped into a
chair, and cried for relief, and she cried, too. He got
himself together to thank me, before she helped him
off to bed, and when she had told her mother and

sister the good news, she came back to me, to ask if she could get me a cup of tea, or something. Her face was so twisted with crying that she could hardly get the words out, and her head went down, down, as if I were some sort of deity, too great and good to look at.

What would *you* have done, Linc? I will tell you what *I* did, and if you will come on here and kick me, I will pay your fare both ways, including sleepers and diners. I took the little fool into my arms, and let her have her cry out on my shoulder, and I took *my* cry out on the top of her yellow head. We did not pass a word, but by and by she lifted up her face and looked into mine, as much as to say that we understood each other, and pulled herself up and kissed me, and then ran out of the room and left me to my thoughts, as they used to do in the novels.

The thoughts have gone on ever since, without any dreams to interrupt. They are to the effect that I am the prize idiot of the universe, and that if I could be wiped out of existence the average of common-sense would be so incalculably increased that this world would be a realm of supernal wisdom. If I am an honest man, if I am any sort of half-way decent scoundrel, I am now bound to this girl, without being the least in love with her, and I have deceived her without meaning her anything but truth.   I *do* like her, Linc; I respect her ; I would rather kill myself than do her harm, and here I have done her the deadliest kind of harm.   Unless all the signs fail, I have either spoiled her peace or mine, forever.   Well, you know me well enough to know that it won't be *her* peace that will suffer.

Yours,

W. A.

XXIII.

From WALLACE ARDITH *to* A. L. WIBBERT, *Wottoma.*

NEW YORK, *Jan. 24, 1902.*

My dear Lincoln:

Your letter has crossed mine, or else you could understand how very little your news can concern me now.   To tell you the truth, I had ceased to be interested in the heart affairs, or no-heart affairs, of a Certain Person some time ago, and now it matters no more to me that she is disengaged than that she was engaged.   The only fact of that kind which makes any appeal to me is my own engagement, which there seems no doubt about, though it is still tacit. It is accepted by the whole Baysley family, of which I seem to be the idol.   The old man is the only one well enough to show me an active adoration, but he is sufficient, and I am not praying for the rapid convalescence of Jenny and her mother.   I suppose they

142

will get well, and then there will have to be something explicit about Essie.

Linc, I don't know what to do. When that child
comes up to me, and expects me to do the lover-like
thing, I have to do it, because I can't bear to
disappoint her; but when she wants me to *say* the
lover-like thing, oh then! It's comparatively easy to
lie with my lips, but when it comes to lying with my
tongue, that is so far beyond the limit, that I don't
know where I am. Upon my word and honor—
honor!—I don't know what I'm saying.

If you haven't guessed anything yet, I will let you
guess now how much I am comforted in getting a
couple of notes a day from America, inquiring about
the Baysleys, and pleading, threatening, to come up
here and look after them herself, if I don't come
down and report. She writes me what you have
written about a Certain Person, and says she is coming on to visit her in March. She adds to the gayety
of nations, as far as I can share it, by joking me
about her, and promising to do everything for me
with her !

Best revise that obituary of mine which you are
keeping in the A box, and add that the subject of the
notice was a youth of so much promise that he

couldn't have done half he said he would if he had lived to be ninety.

Yours ever,

W. A.

You can imagine how nice all this is, coming on top of the chance that Casman has given me in *The Signal*. "Impressions of a Provincial"! If I could make them the Confessions, and make them honest, I should have fame and fortune in my hand, or infamy and misfortune, I don't care which.

XXIV.

From Mr. Otis Binning *to* Mrs. Walter Binning, *Boston.*

New York, *January 24, 1902.*

My dear Margaret;

I am glad to hear you are so much better, but having formed the habit of writing to you, I do not know that I can quite give it up, now, even in the presence of your convalescence. All that I can consent to do is to make my letters shorter, and confine them more to personal interests, leaving out those studies of New York with which I used to pad them. My opportunities, civic and social, continue much the same, though I have indulged rather more than usual in the theatre, that refuge of the society outcast in New York, and I am able to advise you to have yourself carried to see Mrs. Pat Campbell in " The Second Mrs. Tanqueray, " when she brings the play to Boston.

I went to see the piece alone, having declined a

seat in the box of my Cheese and Churn Trust magnate; for knowing the play as I did I hardly saw how
I could talk it over between the acts with his
blooming daughter. Women talk almost anything
with men nowadays, but I do not think a man of my
epoch ought to talk some things over with a girl of
Miss Ralson's. Heaven knows how she and her
young man from Iowa managed the topics suggested
by the play, but perhaps they talked only of themselves—innocent topics enough. I saw her in one of
the chief seats at the spectacle : a box, where she
showed her fine lengths sidewise to the house, and
talked up into the young man's face, with a pictur-
esque slant of her hat. Her father occupied another
chief seat, and the young man stood behind her, and
beside him darkled the quaint girl I have described
to you as her secretary and her mother's companion :
I should like to hear her shrewd comments, but they
are the last thing one is likely to hear, about Mrs.
Tanqueray.

It was a most amusingly New Yorkish crowd that
filled the theatre, dressing pretty much the same for
the boxes and the orchestra places and balconies, and
putting on all possible correctness in the men, and
all fetching hattiness and cloakiness in the women.

I recognized some personalities of social validity, but the rest I took for hotel sojourners, or flat-dwellers of the better sort, or people in successful business, whose supreme society life the theatre party constitutes, shading into presences of harmless Bohemianism—artistic looking art-student girls, in large enough companies to dispense with chaperonage. I wondered how deep some of the awful implications of the play went with those children; but apparently the theatre is only for the surfaces of souls. I fancy most of these amusing New Yorkers were there for Mrs. Pat's acting, and not for the play at all, except as it gave scope to her art and her beauty, and that it was she they talked about between the acts. Not all, however. A German American lady behind me talked incessantly neighborhood gossip of the feeblest and flattest description, passing insensibly from German into English, and from English into German again, without passing the shores of her small beer.

I occupied myself a good deal with the effect of the play in my neighbors, without definite conclusions. I was especially interested in a tall, gaunt figure of a man two vacant seats away, who had Down East written all over his fisherman's face and his clothing-store best; and I decided that he had got there by

mistake.   This proved really to be the case, for when
I made bold to speak to him, as I followed him out
at the end, and to ask him how he liked Mrs. Pat, he
said that he liked her well enough, but had thought
it was going to be some sort of burlesque show, with
dancing.   Then I asked him what he thought of the
play; and he confessed that he did not know whether
he had rightly taken it in.   He could not understand
what it was that made people shy of that Paula, or
what there was in her old acquaintance with her step-
daughter's fellow to make her husband break off the
match, and Paula go and kill herself; but he pre-
sumed it was all right.

I have not seen my pretty boy from Iowa since
that night, though I have been rather diligent in
calling on the daughter of the Cheese and Churn
Trust.   He has not been at the Walhondia for several
days, as I was given to understand, rather airily,
there, yesterday, with an effect of dismissal for the
subject as of great indifference.   I hope no trouble is
brewing, and yet, just for the peculiar interest of the
fact, I should rather like to think he was triffling
with fortune.   He has an enemy, I fancy in the
secretary-companion of Miss Ralson.   Not from anything she said, but from the nothing she looked,

when I mentioned him. She is my enemy, too, I believe, and I am rather sorry for that, for in her queer, angular way, she is charming, with a whimsical tremor round her prim mouth, and in her shy eyes. But I am proud to say that the daughter of the Trust seems to like me, and to be willing to make what she can of me in the absence of the pretty boy. Shall I confess that I amuse myself more in her gorgeous hotel parlor, where no one ever comes that any one knows, than in the hospitalities of the Van der Doeses and their friends? I am afraid I had always a vulgar streak. But do not disown

Your affectionate brother,

OTIS.

XXV.

From Abner J. Baysley *to* Rev. William Baysley,
Timber Creek.

New York, *January 25, 1902.*

Dr. Bro. Wm.:

I'm thankful to say for wife and I that we are about well again. She still keeps her room, but is out of bed, and daughter Jenny is much the same, though not quite so far along as mother. Essie has not been sick at all, and we some hope that she will escape, though we don't want to whistle till we are out of the woods. Will say right here that there never was a better child; and her and young Ardith have about fixed it up together, by the signs. He has been a true friend from first to last, helping Ess do the work like a good fellow when the rest of us was down sick, and using his influence with old Ralson to keep me from being thrown out when I could not get down town to look after things. I got a letter from the company this morning saying my salary was put up to the $3000 notch; so I guess I have been giving satisfaction right along. I did expect to send you a postal order for that loan, but there have been some extra expenses, and I do not believe I can get round to it till next pay day.

Neither Ess or him has said anything yet to me, but from what she told her mother I guess it's a sure thing; and he's as nice a young fellow as ever stepped, and talented. Although he has kept mum about it, I guess he has been pretty thick with the Ralsons. Went into regular Four Hundred circles with them, and them glad to have him. He is not one to brag, and so far as mother can make out, he does not say anything to Ess about it either. But if he was anyways taken up in that direction before, he sticks close enough here now. So it is satisfactory all round.

Hope you are getting the good out of the old place, and glad you can use the horse, riding round. They all join me in regards.

Your affec. bro.,

ABNER.

XXVI.

From WALLACE ARDITH *to* A. L. WIBBERT, *Wottoma.*

NEW YORK, *January 27, 1902.*

Well, my dear Linc, the expected has happened. But where shall I begin to tell you how?

It is more than a week since I called on America, and during that time I have refused three or four invitations from her to breakfast and lunch and dinner, and I don't know what else, each growing a little more formal, and a little less like the good terms we used to be on. All this while I had left her to her own conjectures about my real motives in staying away, for how could I tell her what they were? If I could not understand them, knowing the party as I do, how could she possibly believe in them? But it is dangerous to leave a girl to her conjectures, especially a girl who likes to do her thinking **after she** has done her acting, as most girls do.

152

What America conjectured, as nearly as I can make it out, was that not only all the Baysleys were at the point of death, but that I was not very well myself. The leap from this to the conclusion that it was the part of a friend to come and see what the facts were, was not beyond her powers, and this morning she came. Essie answered the ring from above by pulling the latch of the outside door, and then she had a call from the invalids, some of them, and she ran in where I was writing the "Impressions of a Provincial," and asked if I would stand guard at the door of the apartment, and let in whoever was coming up.

I knew—long before America arrived with her secretary. She began to fill the hallway and staircase with the rich resonance of her laugh, and the proud *frou-frou* of her skirts against the blood-red tapestry carpet, from the moment she came in, while I stood transfixed at the door. She panted, and then laughed at herself for panting, and whispered to the girl with her, and then spoke aloud, and stopped, and came on. Suddenly she stood there on the platform before the Baysley portal, with her skirt in her hand, and the flare from the skylight full in her face, staring at me with a kind of challenge. "Oh!" she said, and the other girl slipped behind her. It was as if she had confronted my ghost, and I wish she had. I could see that somehow she was not prepared for my being there, though why, I could not understand then, even if I understand now. She turned red and then she turned white, but she did not say anything more; she only leaned against the wall, and waited for me. I asked her if she would not come in, and she said "Thank you," in a kind of bewilderment, and she swept in, and the other girl eddied silently in after her. I showed them the way into the horrible little parlor, with the bed-alcove off it, and got them seated, somehow, and then she found presence of mind enough to say, "I hope Mr. and Mrs. Baysley are better." I said they were all better, and Mr. Baysley was so well as to have gone down to the office. I volunteered that Miss Essie Baysley would be with us in a moment, and the conversation languished, till America remarked with the aimlessness of people who don't know what they are saying or saying they don't know what, "I didn't understand that you were living with them, before." I answered that I thought I had mentioned it, and I could see that America suspected I was lying, and that the secretary was making a tacit note of my mendacity. In fact, throughout this glad interview, the secretary had the effect of accumulating evidence against me, I don't know why, and when Essie came in, and I tried to talk to her while America engaged Essie, I felt as if she were warning me that anything I said would be used against me. She has disliked me from the first, apparently, and it hasn't been any better for me because I know she has a conscience against disliking me without reason.

If I had been trying to conceal anything, and certainly I felt as if I were, Essie gave everything away when she came in looking flurried, and then frightened, at the sight of my visitors, if they were mine. In the brief time of our intensified domesticity she has come to depend upon me for pretty much everything but breathing, and now she rubbed kitten-like up against me, with her eyes first on the magnificent America, and then on me, but mostly on me. I was as miserable as a guilty wretch can be, and be conscious of his innocence, but my confounded mind kept taking note of the situation, and in a hideous way rejoicing in it as material. I made out to introduce Essie to the company, and to detach her towards America, while I took the secretary off to the window, and showed her the view of the other side of the street, with the rock in the Park that you can get a glimpse of if you don't mind a crick in your neck. The secretary treated me with merited severity, and gave evidence for the prosecution, and charged the jury, and brought in a verdict of puellicide in the first degree, and sentenced me, and had me in the electric chair, while I saw through the back of my head, all the time, America killing Essie with kindness, and heard her asking her with adamantine benevolence all about the family sickness, and trying to listen, if she died on the spot for it, to Essie's terrified answers. I was actually aware of her holding the girl's hands, and finding them as cold as ice. " Well, you must take care not to get the grippe yourself, " she said, and just then the secretary turned on the current, and I knew no more.

I seemed to come to life in another world, where America and the secretary were talking to Essie, and not minding me any more than if I were an invisible presence. America was saying that she had ventured to bring a few little things to tempt a sick appetite, and that if Essie would let her she would send them up by the man; I noted how she forebore to give Essie the *coup de grâce* by not saying footman. Essie went out to the top of the landing with them, and watched them down the stairs, and then she came back and looked at me. It could not have lasted a long time, but it took a small eternity to live through it, and when it ended in a cloud-burst of tears that seemed to sweep her out of the room, Methusaleh was no match for me in age. I don't know why I waited for the Ralson's James to come up with the hamper America had sent; perhaps I had nothing else to do. I had always been rather friendly with James, but this time I met him with a face as chill as his own imported cheerlessness, and I treated him not like a man, as I had made a point of doing before, but like a footman. He did not seem to notice. Now I am writing to you, and that is all I know.

Your distracted

W. A.

XXVII.

From Miss Ralson *to* Miss Deschenes, *Wottoma.*

Jan. 27, Evening.

Dear Caroline:

I can't remember just what I wrote, but if you understood that I did not want you to come, you must have been reading between the lines. I do want you. Come whenever you like, and as often and as long; you couldn't come too soon, or too much, for me. I really and truly want you, and that's no lie.

I wish I could be decided about Mr. Ardith. But you had better come on and see for yourself. He is living with some people from Timber Creek, up on the West side; I heard that they were all down with the grippe, and I went up to see about them this morning; the father is in the office of the Trust here, and I felt rather obliged to. I don't think they were in much need of me, especially one of the daughters. But I may have been deceived by appearances; you

158

might ask Mr. Ardith after you got here; I will have him to dinner.

I have a bad headache, and I hardly know what I am writing.   Miss Dennam, mother's companion and my secretary, would know if she was here, but she has gone home for the night; so you must try to make it out for yourself.   But if you make out that I don't want you, you will have to settle with me after you get here.

Devotedly yours,

AMERICA.

XXVIII.

From FRANCES DENNAM *to* MRS. DENNAM, *Lake Ridge.*

NEW YORK, *Jan. 27, 1902.*

Dear Mother:

Every now and then I have felt awfully for the way
I have written you about Mr. Ardith: firstly because
he is none of my business, and secondly because I
really care nothing about him, and thirdly because
I don't want to wrong him. You know I wouldn't
hurt a fly, or even a spider that was eating a fly.
Well, I don't know now whether I have been wrong-
ing him, but if I lay the facts fully before you maybe
I shall find out. I can't very well face them till I
get them down on paper, can I?

It seems sort of eavesdropping, but I know that
the drops will go no farther with you and Lizzie, and
so I will keep on, because it is so very interesting, if

for no other reason. The first time I saw him and
Miss Ralson together, I could see that she was perfectly *gone* on him, as you say at Lake Ridge, and the
only thing that I really liked in him was his not being
able to see it. That was certainly in the wretch's
favor; but whether his blindness was a remnant of
the heartbreak (don't mind the mixture of metaphors,
mother!) that he came on here from Wottoma with, I
was not sure. They say that the human male when
heartbroken is easily the prey of the first human female that makes up to him; but in Mr. Ardith's case
the male didn't see it. I don't believe, though, the
female in Miss Ralson's case was fully aware of it, as
I told you in my last letter.

I suppose I have heard more about Mr. Ardith and
his love affair with a Miss Deschenes, out in Wottoma,
than would fill a volume; and from what I could learn,
she behaved as badly to him as I could have wished
in my most venomous moods. She led him on by
every art known to her sex, and then tossed him, as
Miss Ralson said, or gave him the grand bounce, as
she explained. She said Miss Deschenes was very
beautiful in a dark, thin, slight way, and knew how to
dress, far beyond the dreams of Wottoma; she was
very intellectual, too; and nobody could understand

why she turned Mr. Ardith down when it came to the point. The worst of it was that she did not turn him down at once. They were engaged for a while, and then an able lawyer, well along in his thirties, and ripe for Congress, appeared on the scene. This was when the tossing, and bouncing, and turning down took place. In Wattoma it was considered very heartless, and nobody could account for it, but when I met Mr. Ardith, I thought I saw what she meant.

The redeeming feature in his case all along has been his not knowing that Miss Ralson was throwing herself at him. He thought, if he thought anything, that she was binding up his wounds, and perhaps she was, though it looked more like that trapeze act to the outsider. I don't know whether the rest of the family noticed it or not; I rather think not. Mrs. Ralson has seldom seen them together that I know of, and Mr. Ralson's great object seems to have been to see them together as much as possible, or at least to shirk going to places with America and sending Mr. Ardith instead. Where a third person was absolutely demanded by New York propriety, I have done duty, and Mr. Ralson has escaped everything but opera and theatre for the last month. Seven or eight nights ago they were at the theatre together,

and when it was over, they took Mr. Ardith up to his
lodgings, as usual; and they found out that he was
living with some people from the little town in Iowa
where he was born, and that they were mostly down
with the grippe. She thinks he acted very strangely
that night, because he wouldn't let her think of coming to see them, or sending anything; and as the
days have gone by he has acted still more strangely.
He has not come near the Walhondia, and as for
dropping in for lunch, as he had been in the habit
of doing, he would not come when he was asked. I
must say Miss Ralson gave him more chances of re-
fusing than I should have done, and his excuses were
shamefully shallow. Of course I could not say that
to her; and I have done more passive fibbing than I
should have liked to do in the best cause, let alone
one like this. Things went on, Miss Ralson getting
more and more anxious, and vibrating between re-
nouncing him forever, and going to fetch him by
main force. She decided at last that he was down
with the grippe himself, and this morning his condition was so bad, (or hers,) that she could not stand it
any longer. She sent out for a lot of things at a
place where they keep delicacies for the sick, and took
me in her automobile with her to succor the Baysley

family, and to see what the matter with Mr. Ardith really was. She did not say that, of course, but went entirely in the character of an angel of mercy.

I do not know whether she felt like one when she got there, and found Mr. Ardith perfectly well; but I know how *I* should have felt in her place, when the youngest of the Baysley sisters, and the only one on foot, came in and went up to him, and sort of took refuge from her awe of America with him. The situation was quite unmistakable, but I must say that Miss Ralson ignored it magnificently ; and I must say, though I hate to, that he did not quail either, though he looked like death. He left them together and talked with me till Miss Ralson was ready to go, and then he did what was polite, and we got away somehow. But there was no urging him to come down for lunch, or dinner, or breakfast, and there was no mention of him all the way home, except once. She looked out of the window most of the time, and I wonder what people could have thought of her, for when she turned to me, her eyes were simply raining tears. I do not believe she knew it, or was aware of the unnatural voice in which she asked me, "Do you think they are engaged?"

Mother, if we were not so poor, I would have been

willing to give any money not to have had to answer,
and as it is I would have given all Mr. Ralson's
money. But I had to do it. I had to say, "It
seemed to look like it," and then she turned her face
away, and did not speak again. I don't believe she
was mortified at all thinking of how she had given
herself away about Mr. Ardith the other day, and
bragged that she could have him when she wanted.
The hurt was something that went deeper than her
pride, though it came out through that later; now it
was pure heartbreak. I have scarcely seen her, this
afternoon. She had her luncheon taken to her room,
and I had mine with her mother. About four
o'clock she came in to say that if I would like to
go home, then, she would stay with Mrs. Ralson,
and I was glad to get away; but before I could
manage I had to hear her mother afflicting her with
conjectures and questions. She usually does not
notice, but she began at once to ask Miss Ralson
whether Mr. Ardith was sick, and if that was the
reason why he had not been there for so long.
Her daughter fought her off as well as she could,
and told her that Mr. Ardith had been kept by the
sickness of the family he was staying with; that
he had been helping take care of them. Her mother

said, "Well, I always did say he was the best-hearted gentleman I ever saw."

Now, what do you think, mother? For I confess I don't know what to think. Of course if he is in love with that girl, he has a right to be engaged to her, but if he has been in love with her all along, I don't think it was nice in him to come here so much. It is to his credit that he prefers a poor girl, if he really likes her the best, to a rich girl, but I do not understand how any one could like that girl better than America Ralson. For she *is* grand, if she is *rich;* and Miss Baysley struck me as about the commonest piece of prettiness that I ever saw; her grammar was frightful. Propinquity will do much, and he is not to be blamed for being thrown with her in the care of her family. I don't know! The whole thing puzzles me more than it would if it were any of my business, and I don't like to be puzzled, you know. The only thing I am sure of is that Miss Ralson is miserable from it, and that if a man doesn't know enough not to make a girl like her miserable, he ought to; besides it is not very flattering to me, to have a man whom I had set down as a toad turn out something else. The logic of Mr. Ardith ought to have been trifling with that silly

child's affections while he was making love to Miss
Ralson's millions, but he does not seem to have been
doing anything of the kind, unless appearances are
deceiving. Sometimes they are!

> Your affectionate daughter,
>
> FRANCES.

XXIX

From WALLACE ARDITH *to* A. L. WIBBERT, *Wottoma.*

NEW YORK, *Jan'y 28, 1902.*

Dear Lincoln:

Of course I appreciate your friendly advice. If I
were as far off as Wottoma, I have no doubt it would
be perfectly easy for me to act upon it, and I wish to
heaven I were. I might treat with poor Essie
through the long distance telephone, and tell her that
I never really cared for her, and all would be well.
But in this comparative proximity, it is difficult. She
might not understand my motives in the whole
transaction any better than I do. After Miss Ralson
was gone yesterday, Essie kept away from me, and I
made it easy for her by going down town and staying
till the play was over. Then I crept in and began to
write. I expected that she would break in upon me at
first, but nothing worse happened than old Baysley's
visiting me to ask if I knew what ailed Ess, who had

gone to bed crying. I promptly lied to the effect that I did not, and then he stayed to rub the family gratitude into me for what I had done for him with Mr. Ralson, and to say he hoped Ess was not going to be sick, or anything, for he did not know what we should all do. He sat awhile longer in his shirt-sleeves with his stocking-feet against the cooling radiator, and then he left me alone.

I suppose we are not responsible for our thoughts, are we? I should hate to answer for mine, and I don't exactly know what I shall say at the day of judgment when I am asked, How about that little idea that Essie's sickness might not be the worst thing for you? It was as bad as that, Linc, and before I went to bed, I got down on my knees, and prayed to be saved from a thought which, if it was not mine, must have been the devil's own. You may imagine whether I slept very sweetly, but I did sleep, somehow, and I slept late, so late that I did not have the old gentleman's company at breakfast. Essie heard me stirring, and when I came out, she was bringing my coffee and bacon, and her eyes were red and swollen. She put the things down, and then stood hesitating, and looking at me. She sobbed out some kind of pathetic apology to the effect that she didn't mean to offend me, and hoped I was not mad at her: and she knew she was not educated up to me; and not fit for me, anyway, and she would rather die than keep me from being happy.

Isn't life sweet, Linc, and isn't it simple ? Perhaps you will say, off there at Wottoma where things are so easy, that I ought to have reminded her that I had never said, by word of mouth that I loved her, and that so far as I was concerned there was no engagement between us, and she could not make me unhappy, for she had no claim on me whatever. Is that what you would have done ? Perhaps you would, as far off as Wottoma ; but if you had done it here, you would not have been fit to associate even with a miscreant like me.

No, Lincoln, I am in for it, and if the heavenly powers wont help me out, the infernal sha'n't. I go round half-crazy. But if my mind is blurred I shall try to keep my soul clear. Don't take anything amiss that I have said. I do value your interest, and I know your advice is good. The only thing the matter with it is that it is impossible.

Yours ever,

W. A.

XXX

From Mr. Otis Binning *to* Mrs. Walter Binning,
Boston.

New York, *February 5th, 1902.*

Dear Margaret:

I am sorry to hear of your relapse, and I will gladly
do what I can to comfort you with the woes of
others, while you are renewing your care of yourself.
I must say, however, that I cannot respect,—though
I think I could account for it upon a principle which
you would not allow,—your paramount interest in
the affair of Miss Ralson and the pretty boy. It is
very well for you to pretend that these two young
persons are illustrations of New York conditions, but
you must confess, before I go further, that they attract your fancy simply on the old human ground of
their lovership, and that you prefer my writing about
them because, after all, you like gossip better than
anything else in the world. Having extorted this

171

admission from you I do not mind saying that I have
seen very little of them for the last ten days, and
that this little has been very unsatisfactory. Your
young man, in fact, I have not seen at all, and your
young woman I have seen only in the most cursory
manner. This has not been for want of trying. I
have called several times at the Walhondia, but each
time Miss Ralson has been out, or been out of repair;
and when I have found her in, but ill, I have had to
console myself as I could with her secretary, Miss
Dennam. You will say that you care to hear nothing
of Miss Dennam, and I can only say I am sorry you
don't, for I am sure if you could have seen the sort
of conscientious tolerance of me, which marks the
present extreme of her kindness, growing upon her,
you would have been amused; and I think you would
have admired the art with which I tried to convince
her that I was not the heartless old worldling she
had set me down for. I can feel that she has con-
tested with herself every inch of the way to a better
opinion of me. I believe she formerly regarded me
as a sort of emissary from the mythical Four
Hundred sent to beguile Miss Ralson, and bring her
into its toils bereft of self-respect and the flower of
her native ingenuousness. But now, if Miss Dennam

still despises me, she also pities me ; she has consented to talk with me, and has not altogether refused to
satisfy a curiosity I betrayed concerning the civilization of Lake Ridge. She seems a survival of the old
New England morality, and I was not surprised to
find that she was of a New England stock, flourishing the more vigorously from its transplantation to
western New York. Something ancestral in me
sympathized with what I divined of her, while posterity as I represent it, kept itself with difficulty from
smiling at her pathetic casuistries in the matters I
made bold to touch on. I know you are impatient
of this, Margaret, and yet I think you would have
enjoyed the psychological spectacle, especially when
I entered upon some question of Mr. Ardith, which I
ventured to do, very, very discreetly after I found
there was to be no question whatever of Miss Ralson.
Her face involuntarily lighted up at my asking if she
had seen him lately, and then darkened again as she
answered, " Not for a week : " I could see her men-
tally making scrupulous count of the days, so as not
sin against him by the smallest excess. I expressed
the hope that he was well, and she answered that
when they saw him he was well. Then I went so far
as to say that he had a face which had interested me

rather, from the first, as having a certain strength in spite of his apparent physical delicacy, which promised success for him; and she shot out, as if without intending it, that he seemed the kind of person who would probably get what he wanted in life.

I asked her if she would mind telling me just what she meant by that, and she said that she thought she had already expressed her meaning. Then I suggested, "You mean that he is selfish?" and I added that I had known some selfish people who had no more got what they wanted than some unselfish people. She protested that she did not mean to say Mr. Ardith was more selfish than others. He was very ambitious, and he was talented; and had I read any of his things? He was writing for the *Signal* now. She offered to get me a copy of the paper, if I liked; but I was afraid she wished to leave the subject, and I detained her with another question of psychological import. I began with the fact that from the first I had felt the attraction of something finally innocent in Mr. Ardith's face, perhaps the air of one who could make sacrifices; and I proposed the inquiry whether we had always the grounds in ourselves for judging others. "Have I been judging him?" she wanted to know, and of course I answered, "Not in

the least. I was thinking merely how outside of the
current youth my age seemed to leave me, " and she
made the instant reflection that a woman was always
disabled from judging men, young or old, because
she was a woman. I admitted that this was probably
the case, and then I put before her a dissatisfaction I
am beginning to experience with my judgments of
New York, which I perceive more and more to be
upon the Boston grounds, when they ought to be
upon the New York grounds, if they are to have any
value. That made her laugh, and she explained her
laughing as from a sudden realization of the possibil-
ity that she had been judging New York on Lake
Ridge grounds. She would not explain what these
were, but promised sometime to do so if I would explain the Boston grounds. I offered to illustrate
them by saying that in our Boston solar system the
meteoric visitors that roam harmlessly through the
spacious New York firmament would jar social
planets of the first magnitude, and impart a thrill of
anxious question to the whole social framework; but
as if she felt a slant towards Miss Ralson in this, she
refused to go farther, and although I believed that I
had left her curious, I could be certain only that I
had left her silent.

I tried boldly, for your sake, to discuss Miss Ralson in plain terms, but Miss Dennam would have none of it. When I ventured some analytical appreciations of the Trust himself, she did not refuse to join me, though again at my conjectures as to whether his charming daughter was more like her mother than like the Trust, I was aware of being delicately but firmly withheld. It was as if Miss Dennam's loyalty included reservations such as a person of more than Lake Ridge experiences might have had, and she was defending the Ralson family from herself as well as from me. Yet, in spite of her, and rather from her repression than from her expression, I fancied—always in your interest, Margaret!—that there was some sort of trouble in the Ralson household, and that this was mystically related to the retrorsive Mr. Ardith. I have imagined—still in your interest!—that the beautiful America—that is really her spacious name; in the West they seem to require names of continental implication—has felt the charm that I have found in Mr. Ardith, without perhaps being able to make him responsive to her feeling. It would be a novel and fascinating situation, would not it? To have a beautiful millionairess in love with a poor young journalist, and to have the poor young journalist hesitating, or possibly not hesitating, about denying himself the boon fortune: that would be something so original as almost to be aboriginal. But what I want you to own, Margaret, is that I could not have done more handsomely by the leisure into which you have relapsed, or supplied you with a richer feast of surmise.

Your affectionate brother,

OTIS.

XXXI.

From WALLACE ARDITH *to* A. L. WIBBERT, *Wottoma.*

NEW YORK, *Feb. 6, 1902.*

My dear Lincoln:

I hesitate to tell you what has happened, but of course I am going to do it.

As long as I could, I made an excuse to myself of the Baysleys' sickness for not going to see the Ralsons, or rather America; but to you I will lie as little about it as I can. When the other Baysleys had got well enough to do their own work, and Essie had not taken the grippe from the others, I had no excuse even with myself for staying away. You might say that common decency might still have been my excuse, but my experience is that common decency has nothing to do with affairs of the heart. Besides there was nothing explicit about the situation, and I had a feeling that it was rather loutish to let it make a break in the friendship between us; I

mean between America and me.   I was bound to
ignore it, and ignore it actively as well as passively.
So I went down to the Walhondia this afternoon, and
sent up my name to the family; sometimes Mrs. Ralson likes to see me when America is out.

There was a longer hesitation in the bell-boy than
usual, and I was beginning to be afraid he had got
lost when he came back and said the ladies wished
me to come up.   I don't believe the elevator ever took
up a heavier load, but it got me to their floor without
breaking down, and the maid let me in, as usual.
While I waited, I perused the roofs of the city, and
found a curious interest in impaling myself on a
church steeple about fifty feet below the Ralsons' windows.   Then I heard a sort of shy stir behind me, and
I knew that it was my enemy, the secretary, who had
come into the drawing-room.   I don't know why that
girl should hate me unless it is because she divines
me, and I don't know why I should hate her, for I
entirely agree with her in her objections to me.   But
she was civil enough, and asked me to sit down, as if
nothing had happened, since I was there the last time,
to prevent it.   She said Miss Ralson was not very
well and was sorry she should not be able to see me,
but that Mrs. Ralson had heard I was below and had

wished me to come up. I said that was very kind of
Mrs. Ralson, and I should like to see her and I hoped
there was nothing serious the matter with Miss Ralson; of course I knew there was not, and Miss
Dennam made my assurance doubly sure. After a
little more skirmishing she got up, and said she
would go and see if Mrs. Ralson were ready, for she
would like me to come into her room, if I would
not mind.

She went out, and I went back and re-impaled myself on the steeple, and this time when the door
opened from the inner room, I knew it was not Miss
Dennam who was returning. I knew that it was
America who was sweeping toward me, and I felt the
sort of authority that suppressed indignation lends a
girl's movement, in her swift progress towards my
back. I faced about promptly, and put on as good a
front as I could, though my heart was in my boots;
but I left her the initiative. She was equal to it, and
towered down upon me with an out-stretched hand.
She said, "How do you do?" with all her robust
presence, and there was not a moment's fooling with
the question of her not being well. I never saw her
look better, and she was the more splendid for being
mad through and through with me. (I speak with

the light that subsequent events threw back upon the fact.)   She said it was very kind of me to come when I must be so anxious about my friends; but perhaps there was no reason to be anxious about them any longer?   She hoped they were better, and that that poor little thing had not worked herself to death taking care of the others: such a frail-looking little thing!   I knew that she meant Essie, and I said that the whole Baysley family were convalescent, and the poor little thing was none the worse for her care of them.   She did not appear to have noticed anything that did not refer to Essie, but to that she said, "Of course, you would see that she didn't overdo.   She told me how you had helped her."

I had nothing in particular to answer, except to disown having done anything, and we talked a lot of inanities, and then I got up to go; I had quite forgotten her mother.   She seemed to have forgotten her too, for she merely said, Oh, must I go so soon? and followed me to the door, where she put out her hand again, and suggested, "I don't know whether you will allow me to congratulate you, Mr. Ardith?"   I knew very well what she meant, but I got back with the established formula that we use when we know perfectly well what people mean: "I don't know what you mean." "I beg your pardon for being indis-creet," she said, and then I said, "I don't know what you mean," again. "I am quite willing to be con-gratulated upon anything there is cause for." "On your engagement to Miss Baysley, for instance?" she suggested. She tried to be arch, about it, but she smiled with her lips, not with her eyes, and I saw her chin tremble. I got the words up from some-where inside of me, "I am not engaged to Miss Bays-ley," and I waited for the next thing with a perfect quiet. One *is* quiet when one is dead, and I was dead at that moment.

She took a good long look at me, and we seemed tranced together in an endless moment. She gasped, "Not—engaged!" "Certainly not to Miss Baysley," I answered; but I did not add that, if I was not, I was a scoundrel. When you begin a bluff of that kind you have to go on, and I went on, "I am in love with some one else," and again we held each other with a look. "Oh! Did you know she was coming here,—Miss Deschenes?" We had never mentioned her since that first night we were at the theatre to-gether, and there must have been a great stress on her to make her do it now. I said, "No, I didn't know. But I didn't mean Miss Deschenes. I meant you."

It was as if I had dealt her some kind of blinding stroke. She drooped forward with her left hand to her eyes, while she put out the other to me, as if to keep herself from reeling. She said, "Come!" and pulled me back into the room. " Now tell me what you mean ! "

There would be a white line here if it were fiction, but it is fact, and I must ask you to imagine the rest without giving you a white line to do it in. I stayed down there the whole afternoon, then to dinner and then far into the evening. Now I am here, facing another order of realities, or rather fighting away from facing them. Every moment I expect Essie to come in for an explanation of my long absence, and consolation. She will come in, and hang upon me; and shall I deal as frankly with her as I dealt with America? Can a man be frank with two women at a time? I could make America understand how, without a promise from me, without one word of love-making, this poor girl should have come to look upon me as belonging to her, and should trust in me as wholly as if I had asked her in absolute terms to be my wife. And I do respect her, Linc; I do like her. She is an ignorant little thing, but she is true, and she is not vulgar,—not like me, who feel myself false to the

finger tips, and vulgar to the bottom of my mean
soul.   While I was with America, I was safe.   I accounted for myself, I justified myself, or else I let her
do it for me, on condition that I would tell Essie
everything at once.   But now that I am away from
her, I am afraid, and all my fine, bold pretences and
purposes have tumbled into chaos.   Not yours, for
you won't own me after this, but the devil's own

W. A.

P. S.   Jennie Baysley has just been in to tell me
that Essie is down with the grippe, and they are afraid
she is very bad.   They want me to go for the doctor.

XXXII.

New York, *February the sixth, One thousand nine hundred and two.*

My dear Caroline:

I do not know where to begin, and so I will begin in the middle. Mr. Ardith and I are engaged, and the circumstances are such that I think you ought to be the very first to know it, outside of my own family. It happened this afternoon, quite out of a clear sky, though I guess there must have been an electrical disturbance somewhere ever since we met here in December. The disturbance was increased by something I imagined, the other day, and there has been a very low pressure in the region of the heart for the whole week past. But now it is all over, and I am so happy! He has been so brave in explaining everything away; he is the soul of truth and honor, and if I had always understood the literary temperament as well as I do now, I would never have had the least anxiety.

It may seem rather heartless for me to be parading this before you, Caro, but I do not believe you ever really cared for him, or you would not have given him up; and now if I don't let you have a second chance you can't blame me, exactly, can you? My first idea was, " Now I must write to Caro Deschenes, and take back that invitation, " but I am not going to take it back, and you must come the same as ever. We haven't either of us done anything to be ashamed of, have we? Any way, *I'm* not ashamed, and you must come and help me brazen it out. That is what we both think, Wallace and I, and he joins me in wishing to see you again, and in asking your blessing. I can't exactly ask you to come and be my bridesmaid, for we haven't got quite so far along as that, yet, but if you will come and visit me, you will be a ministering angel. I will not write the great news to any one else in Wottoma, and I will ask you not to say anything just at present. My, but what a chapter for the Sunday edition of the *Day!* If they come to you for a photograph, I wish you would give them that one with the lifted profile—the one with

the Madonna look. Mr. Wibbert has got lots of
Wallace. With all the love I can spare from him,

Yours devotedly,

AMERICA.

XXXIII.

From WALLACE A. ARDITH *to* A. L. WIBBERT, *Wottoma.*

NEW YORK, *Feb. 7th, 1902.*

Dear Lincoln :

I feel that I left you at the close of an exciting
installment last night, as if I were writing some
wretched romance, instead of this wretched reality.
I posted my letter on the way to the doctor, who
found things not so bad as they had looked to the
family, but it is a severe case, with the peculiarities
of the sudden sort of seizure. As I cannot go to the
sick room, I am rather left out of it; and what do
you think ? I have spent the morning, while waiting
to be sent on errands, and doing odd jobs about the
house, in writing more " Impressions of a Provincial"
for the *Signal!* How strangely we are made, we who
are born to scribble! I feel a sort of disgrace in it,
but it is not as bad as the other sort of disgrace I
feel, and it is a change, any way.

I was to have gone down to the Walhondia this morning, to breakfast there, but I had to send a note instead. I was afraid it would bring America back with it, on one of her magnificent impulses, but women's instincts are to be trusted in these matters. She merely answered me with a note of beautiful sympathy (that made me want to have the mountains fall on me,) and forbade me to think of coming near her if I could be of the least use in the world here. But I had better go, and I shall, as soon as old Baysley gets home this afternoon; there ought to be some man about, here. I beg his pardon for calling him old Baysley; my light-hearted disrespect for him is gone, along with the rest of my light-heartedness. I can only pity the poor old fellow, and hope that I am not pitying myself at the same time. I will keep you posted, of course.

Yours ever,

W. A.

XXXIV.

From Mr. Otis Binning *to* Mrs. Walter Binning,
Boston.

New York, *February 14, 1902.*

My Dear Margaret:

In writing the date of this letter I have realized
what day it is, and I venture to offer myself for your
Valentine: I do not believe Wally will really mind
much.

As a metropolis we are in tiptoe expectation of
Prince Henry's coming, and if we can believe the
newspapers, which we never can, our businesses and
bosoms are penetrated with a generous impatience,
alloyed by no base respect of persons, or love of
royalties, but inspired solely by a hitherto unimag-
ined sympathy for the great German people and their
magnanimous ruler. Some of us do not see quite
how we are going to express this in the municipal
reception of a representative who was born and not

chosen for the business, but we are going to try, on a scale never before attempted. You will read all that in the public prints, and I have nothing subjective to offer you concerning it. If there is anything that really interests or amuses me it is the fact that while this storm is going on in the newspapers, the depths of our life are quite unstirred by it. We read of the Prince's coming, and perhaps we fleetingly think of it, but, in a wonderful measure, nobody speaks of it. We are queer, we Americans, and if any one takes up the study of us in that dark future when we shall have ceased to be Americans, he will find the New Yorkers, and not the frontiersmen, the queerest Americans of all. In fact the New Yorkers *are* the frontiersmen, as I will explain to you, some day; but now the postulate would be too exhausting to handle.

I usually have a nap in a secluded armchair at the club after lunch, and then I cross the dangerous trolley lines for a stroll into the Park. In common with a great many other very young and very old people, I make it a large part of my business there to feed the squirrels, which are of a tameness curiously flattering to human pride. Privately, I think the squirrel is an extremely stupid little beast, with but small and imperfect use of even such minor perceptive faculties as seeing and hearing. But when, after starting up on his hind feet, and holding his forearms pressed to his throbbing breast, he makes me out at a little distance, and comes loping across the grass to get the nut I am holding out to him, I feel very much as I think I should if a great beauty should mistake me for a splendid youth, or Prince Henry should shake hands with me. It seems to single me out from my race as worthy the Creator's peculiar confidence, which this small creature is commissioned to express; and though I see plenty of other squirrels making for nuts held out to them by other men, the fact does not affect my self-approval; I am still singly our Creator's choice. In fact I think I have some really special reason to be satisfied with myself, for in the Ramble there is one squirrel who is my personal acquaintance: not because I think he knows me, for I doubt it, but because I know him, though I should not know him by his mental or moral difference from other squirrels so much as by the fact that one of his paws has been hurt, perhaps in the day of—

—" Old, unhappy, far-off things,
And battles long ago."

The scar may be from a wound received in the worst of causes, but it serves: it distinguishes that squirrel,

and gives him a limp to which my imagination bows.
I am not sure that it does not make him cross; at
any rate he is rather bad-tempered, and he does me
the honor, when he climbs upon my knee, to bite my
finger if I am slow in getting out the kernels of the
nuts I give him. He prefers them crumbled up, and
he noses for them in my palm like a minute pig.
This gives me a delight which the cleanest conscience
could not impart. I glow with the most agreeable
self-righteousness, and I am aware of smiling in my
rapture like a sinner who has made sure of the forgiveness he has been rather uncertain of.

This afternoon I found my squirrel, or my squirrel
found me, with unusual ease in the Ramble, and I
was sitting with him on my knee, feeding him
crumbled peanuts (he prefers peanuts) and rejoicing
in the excellent terms which I was on with my Maker
through some merit of mine which that sagacious an-
imal had divined, when I was sensible of being rather
steadily gazed at. Steps had paused a little way
from me and I surmised another squirrel amateur: we
often stop to look at one another and envy one
another in moments of high success. I enjoyed my
triumph for a due space, and then I looked up to
meet the gaze which I felt, and found that it was my

pretty boy from Iowa who was looking at me. I dare say he would have respected my preoccupation with superior interests, and passed on, but just then the squirrel finished the last morsel of his peanuts, and ran away. This allowed me to give Mr. Ardith a less divided inspection, and I discovered such tragedy in his face as I have not often seen off the stage. What will you say, Margaret, when I declare that I discovered there a hardy cynicism, mixed with a fine grief, and an utter despondency, such as one does not often find in the human countenance even *on* the stage? But I know you will say that I discovered them there after he told me what was the matter.

The strange part is that he did not tell me. I asked him how he did, and he answered that he did very well, and while he informed himself of my health, I made room for him on my bench, and invited him to sit down. The day was so mild, and I was so well wrapped up that I did not mind his taking cold if he chose to risk it ; in fact I was not conscious of his seeming rather pale and pinched till afterwards. He sat down, and told me that we had met first in that place, and I said, " Oh, yes, yes, " till he reminded me of an incident which I had forgotten, but which he seemed to have valued greatly. It was of two young lovers whom we had happened to notice, walking up toward that colossal bust of Schiller, which you may remember here, in a turn of the path by the lake with their arms round each other. They glanced back and saw us, and their arms dropped. Then the young girl in a brave defiance, made a fine rush at her lover, and flung her arm about him again, and so they passed from our sight into the nook beyond the bust. My youth and I had some banter about the little episode, and at his saying it ought to go into a poem, I suggested putting it into a play. But the thing quite went out of my mind, and though when I next met the Iowa youth, I was teased with the sense of having met him before, I took it for one of those intimations of pre-existance which are rather commoner with us as we get on in life than the intimations of post-existence. I now said, " Well, I suppose they are still *liebing* and *lebing*, " with Schiller's line about having done so, in my mind. "Have you got them into a poem yet ? " He said, " No more than you in a play, I suppose. " I confessed that I had not immortalized them in drama, and then I suggested that it was perhaps as well to leave them in life, and at that he dropped his head, with a sigh, and said, " Oh, yes; but if it was a mistake of theirs, literature could have helped them out of it much easier than life could."

This notion, together with the sigh, interested me, and I scented a bit of psychology that I might purvey to you. "Then you think," I said, "that such things are sometimes mistakes?" and "Aren't they usually?" he asked. I said, "Well, that is what they are supposed to be in the first blossoming of the affections," and he asked again, "The affections are supposed to learn wisdom for the second or third blossoming?" This would have been a sneer, if it had not been so sad, and I did not pounce upon the young man for it, as, for instance, you would have done. I merely said, "That is the accepted attitude toward such matters. Then you think

'They are false guides, the affections,'

in affairs of the heart?" I claimed that I was quite disinterested in the inquiry, for I was past making a selfish use of any wisdom on the subject that he happened to have. My young man laughed rather desolately, and said the affections seemed to be of so many minds, and perhaps that was the reason why people of experience distrusted them, and thought them false when they were really sincere in their

devotion to several objects. I said that was rather
interesting, but I asked, " Was it true?" He allowed
that it might not be true, and put the burden on me
of saying whether it was so or not. I confess that
in a swift review of my past, I seemed to find some
proofs of his theory, but I said that in all such cases
I thought I remembered a supreme goddess of my
idolatry, though there might be other demi-god-
desses at the same time. I expressed my surprise
that the fact had never been adequately treated in
literature, and he answered bitterly that life had
never been adequately treated in literature, either because life was too bold, or because literature was too
timid.

It seemed to me that this was a point at which I
could becomingly put on the moralist with one so
much my junior, and I intimated that the man who
imagined himself in love with several women at the
same time would do well to examine himself for the
question whether he was not solely in love with himself. To my surprise, he was not daunted by my
attitude, " Yes," he said, "such a man might be a
rascal, and yet he might be least a rascal in the
reality of his varied preference. His only excuse for
liking one woman for one thing, and another woman

for another reason, would be the honesty of his liking. " " Well, my dear young friend, " I answered, " I should much rather contemplate such a predicament in literature than in life. In literature, I might be psychologically interested in him, or the author's skill in working him out, but in life, I am afraid I should wish to kick him. " My mind was playing with the thought of that glowing daughter of the Trust whom I have seen so much with this Mr. Ardith, and I was wondering if he were associating some inferior deity with her in the worship which I have fancied him paying her. I thought it as well to let him know how a dispassionate witness would feel in such an event; but he was not crushed, or at least not silenced by my severity. " The man might wish to kick himself," he said, " and yet he might feel a mystery in the affair which the spectator couldn't, and he might feel that the mystery was something for which kicking was not the just meed. Perhaps the author who treated him in literature would do well to take into account a genuine shame in him for what was so adverse to the general acceptations in such matters; they can't be called convictions. " His courage interested me, Margaret, and I asked with a tolerence which I hope you won't call disgraceful.

"How would you justify him?" He answered, "I wouldn't justify him; I would ascertain him," and I thought that neat, if not acute, which I also thought it. "I would find out whether his condition was a real psychological condition, or whether it was only the sort of hallucination which the mere horror of a thing sometimes produces in us, and makes us feel as if it were 'founded on fact.'" I could not deny that this was a very pretty conjecture, and I did not. "For literature?" he pursued. "Prettier than for life," I said, and I said also that the thing might merit inquiry in life, too, where the first business of the inquirer would be to find out whether the fellow was not a plain rascal. He consented to that, and I went on. "Such a case I should think might very well be submitted to 'the finer female sense' that Tennyson believes more easily offended than ours." Then I thought I might fitly cover all the possibilities while I was about it. "If it were a case in real life, the fellow couldn't do better than go with it to some woman whom he suspected of not liking him. Then he would be apt to get an opinion worth having. And if it were a case in literature, he couldn't have better criticism than such a woman's mind."

To be quite honest, I had begun to fancy something unwholesome in the young man, and I was now willing to defend myself from him at the cost of hurting him. I did not like the direction the conversation had taken, but I don't say this was very handsome of me; I had led him on to talk freely, and I was making a personal affair of what might be quite an abstraction. He sat still without saying anything, and then he sneezed violently three times. This made me look at him, and I saw that he was wearing a fall overcoat; he shivered, and I said, "Aren't you made up rather lightly for this evening air?" and he answered that he had put on that coat earlier in the afternoon, and had got warm with walking, but now he did feel the chill. He rose to take leave of me, and I put out my hand to shake his; it was cold. "You must look out for the grippe," I said, and he answered, "I've been living with it for the last three or four weeks. The people where I lodge have all been down with it one after another, like a row of bricks."

He lifted his hat, and went off down the walk away from the Schiller, and as he went I followed him with a forgiving pathos which I hope you will share, Margaret.

Yours affectionately,

OTIS.

XXXV

New York, *Feb. 14, 1902.*

My Dear Mother:

I want to tell you to begin with, that I feel as if all my principles had been pulled up by the roots, and flung out on the woodpile in the back yard, like old geraniums that had failed to do their duty indoors, and did not deserve anything better. I haven't got a single principle left, and though I am not imme-diately concerned, I feel that I have no dependence but Providence, in case anything should happen.

I wrote you about the call which Miss Ralson made me make with her at the Baysleys' to see what had become of Mr. Ardith; and I told you that we *saw* what, only too distinctly. But that seems to have been an optical delusion. Mr. Ardith certainly ap-peared to be engaged to the youngest Miss Baysley,

but if we are to believe subsequent events, he was not
engaged to her in the least. A week after we had
settled down to our mistake, Mr. Ardith called, and
asked for the ladies. This gave Miss Ralson a chance
to say that she was sick, or something, but her mother
had heard his name, and she insisted on having him
come up. I received him, and then while I went in
to make Mrs. Ralson up for company—I mean moral-
ly, for physically the maid looks after her, of course—
Miss Ralson found that she could and would see him,
and she did. What took place I shall probably never
know in detail, but when I came back to get Mr. Ardith for her mother, he was gone, and Miss Ralson
astounded me by grappling my unyielding form to her
heart, and announcing that she was engaged to Mr.
Ardith. She said that sometime she would tell me
about it, but that now she merely wanted to celebrate,
and she went on with a celebration in which Mr. Ardith was proclaimed the noblest and wisest and best
of his sex. He seemed to have achieved his pre-
eminence by having told her that he was not in love
with the youngest Miss Baysley, but only and always
with herself, and that the appearances which were so
much against this theory could be easily accounted
for on the ground that he had felt very sorry for Miss

Baysley in her trials with her sick family, and had befriended her in every way he could, to the extent of helping her with the housework, but he had never told her that he cared for her, and he was not responsible for her thinking he did, if she thought so.

I must say, mother, that when Miss Ralson got that off to me, I felt that Mr. Ardith deserved all my original disapprobation, but I could not say so to Miss Ralson. I was so indignant I could hardly speak, but if I could have spoken I had no business to tell her that I always believed he was a heartless little wretch, and now I believed he was a wicked traitor. I wanted to fly out and declare that such a simpleton as that poor girl even, could not be so self-deluded as to think he cared for her, if he had not looked it and acted it, and that his not saying it did not matter. But I held in, and Miss Ralson went on, and did not notice my coolness, except to say that I was not celebrating worth a cent, and to laugh at what she considered my reserved nature. The most that I could do was to intimate that she would want to tell her father and mother at once, and then she said, No, she and Mr. Ardith had agreed to let it go, a little while, and it was to be a dead secret between her and me. She said it would be all right with her father and mother, whenever she told them, for they were both as much in love with Mr. Ardith as she was; and I could not deny that. Mrs. Ralson has been quite frank about it from the beginning with me, and has always hoped that Make would take a fancy to him, and Mr. Ralson has done everything that an entire resignation of his paternal duties to Mr. Ardith could do to show him that there would be no trouble when he wanted to assume any filial duties. Ever since Mr. Ardith has been coming here there has been a sort of lull in Miss Ralson's social campaign, and I think her father has felt it such a blessed respite that he has been willing to prolong it on any terms. He has not had to go with her to any of the functions where she used to drag him, and she has left off a great many of them herself.

It was a week ago that she told me of her engagement, and he has been here a part of every day since, and I must say that he has seemed very much in love with her. They have kept up a pretty lively interchange of notes, and I have had to be consulted on many of the letters and answers; in fact I have had to help compose some of the answers, for Miss Ralson has held that she ought to make them the nicest kind, and as nearly up to his as possible. Sometimes I have wanted to resign and clear out altogether, for I could not approve of the affair as it stood, and I felt that if I was abetting it I was doing a thing that my conscience would give me gowdy for sooner or later. He has been staying on with the Baysleys, and has made an excuse of that girl's having the grippe herself now for not leaving them. I don't understand that he is actually helping nurse her, but the family have got to depending on him so that he cannot leave them. That is the prose of it, and what the poetry of it is that he makes up for Miss Ralson, I don't know, of course; I have kept away from their poetry as much as I could; but any sort of doggerel would do for Miss Ralson in the state she is in. I don't mean to say that he has been dishonest with her, about the Baysley girl, but if he had wanted to be, Miss Ralson has offered him every inducement by her blind faith in him. Any old thing that he chose to say would have gone with her. Her only trouble was that she couldn't go and be with him, when he couldn't come and be with her.

I don't know whether this is preparing you for what has just happened or not, or whether anything could prepare you; nothing could have prepared *me*, I know. Mr. Ardith has been here, and he has left me in a state of mind that is worse than *no* mind. He asked for me, but I should not have been allowed to see him more than a minute alone if Miss Ralson had been at home; she happened to be out, and so I had the strange visit quite to myself. For an accepted lover, he has looked more excited than happy during the whole time since she announced their engagement to me, but when he came in to-day, he looked ghastly. He hardly took time to say how do you do, before he began on the business that apparently filled him to the brim.

He opened with the surprising remark, "I know you don't like me, Miss Dennam." I was not going to deny a thing of that kind, even if it were true, and so I smiled, and asked how he had happened to find out my secret; but he would not have any fooling. He said, "No matter; I know it, and I have come to you because I know it." He stopped, and I just waited. "I have always felt that you were disposed to judge me severely, and now I want all the severity you can give my case. If I have been letting myself up too easily, I know you won't abet me." Of course, I suspected that this had something to do with his engagement to Miss Ralson, but still I did not say anything, and he went on again. "I saw what you

thought that day at the Baysleys', and now I have
come to say that up to a certain point, you were right.
I want to make a clean breast of it, if a breast like
mine can be made clean, and to tell you that in a
kind of way I did care for that poor girl." "Excuse
me, Mr. Ardith," I said, "I would rather you would
not tell me this. I don't want to know about your
affairs." But that was not the truth, and you know
it, mother, and perhaps he saw it. At any rate he
went on, just as if I had been dying, as I really was,
to hear about his affairs.

He said, "I can't help that: you have got to hear
about them. The fact that you have always distrusted
me has given me the right to *make* you hear, for you
are the one person who can see these things in the
true light, and do me justice." He tried to keep
quiet but he was trembling with excitement, and he
looked fairly sick. "You know that whether I cared
for her or not, she cared for me, and now you know
that I have been telling America that I care for *her*.
I do care for her—the whole world. She is the best
and dearest thing in it to me; and yet I care for that
other—too. I don't defend myself, and if I try to
explain myself it's because—because I want to see if
you can understand me. Sometimes it seems to me

that I must be insane. My mind keeps working on
that one point, and can't leave it. I have thought
that a word of blame, a verdict of guilty, would kill
me. But now I believe that it is the only thing that
can save me. And I've come to you for it; but I
won't let you think that I have meant any harm. I
haven't. I came to New York after a wretched business in Wottoma which I know you know about, and
I have been in love with America ever since I saw her
here, the first night, and I realized how good and
beautiful she was: I had never known it before, but
the time had come. Well, I got in with those people—the people I am living with—and I can say that
I helped them in their helplessness. It was what anybody would have done under the same circumstances.
They were from the town where I was born, and they
were poor, and pretty soon they were sick, all but that
girl. I don't know whether she cared for me, at first,
and it may have been my being friendly that made
her. But I saw it coming, and I liked it—yes, I did!
though I was in love with America then as much as
I could be. I haven't wronged the girl by one word
of love-making, but I know she thinks I am in love
with her. There you have the whole case—or not
the whole, either. The others have had the grippe

and got over it. Now she has it. At first I thought
she was going to die, and—but she is getting better,
though she is still very sick. The rest have taken
care of her, of course, and my part has been what it
is, yet, to keep up the ghastly fraud. But it isn't
altogether a fraud. I do like her—not as I like
America, but as I can't help liking any creature that
likes me—that has trusted me. Oh! I know what my
duty is! My duty is to tell her that I don't care for
her as she cares for me, to kill her with that, and then
come and tell America that our engagement must be
off because I have liked some one else while I was
loving her. But I am not going to do either. I am
going away." He stopped, and while I still couldn't
make any reply, he went on: "When I began, I
thought I wanted to know what you would say. But
now I don't. It wouldn't matter what you said. It
couldn't make it any better if you justified me at
every point, and it couldn't make it worse if you con-
demned me."

He got up, and began gathering his overcoat into
his arm, and letting it drop, and then taking it up
again, and he did not seem to know what he was
doing, but he went toward the door, while I tried to
gasp out something. And do you know what it was

I gasped out, when it came? It was this: that I was sorry for him, and that if I had never believed in him before I believed in him now; and I begged him to tell Miss Ralson what he had told me, or if he couldn't, to let me tell her; for I knew that she would take it in the right way, she was so large-minded and so noble and good. I forgot how I had always accused him in my own mind of being a sneak, and then of being a traitor, and had suspected him of deserting that Baysley girl because she was poor, and of trying to get Miss Ralson because she was rich; and now, simply because he had confessed the worst things about himself that a man could, I was trying to comfort him, and encourage him, and make him think that it was not such a desperate case, after all. He listened to me, in a sort of daze, and then as if he had realized what I was saying he fairly laughed in my face, and ran out of the room.

Now, what do you say, mother? Have I gone clear, stark, raving distracted, or is there something in what he said? I suppose that nobody but a man would know, and yet I don't believe that any one but a woman could judge him fairly, and that is why my principles are out on the woodpile in the backyard. Don't you see that if we let men go on at that rate, it would excuse every kind of wicked flirtation, and I don't know but polygamy itself? I don't know what the end of it will be or what anybody can do about it. I can't tell whether I ought to let Miss Ralson know about it, or just leave it to fate, or nature, or Providence. It might be the best thing if he did go away, the best thing for her and for that wretched Baysley girl, not to mention your own bewildered daughter.

FRANCES.

XXXVI.

From W. Ardith *to* A. L. Wibbert, *Wottoma.*

New York, *Feb. 14, 1902.*

My dear Linc.

I guess I am going in for it; no one ever knows how the grippe is going to end, but I could tell you how it begins. My head is like lead, but through this density, the queerest little antic deliriums go capering as nimbly as if it were the finest ether; if I could note them down, or remember them for future use, they would be the weirdest sort of material.

I want to tell you something, but I do not know what it is long enough to get it out. It is something about that girl who secretaries and companions for the Ralsons; I shall have it directly; never mind. That old Boston cock up in the Park, feeding the squirrels, where I first saw him, near the bust of Schiller, had something to do with it. America was not there —

212

Lord, how it keeps escaping me! But I shall get it, and I shall keep on writing.

I should like to make a fight of it, everyway, and see how long I could beat the thing off. I wonder if a man could give a thing of that sort the worst of it, if he held on to his courage. If my legs were good for it, I would go out, and walk it off. But my confounded legs won't work. It is only the upper half of me that seems to have any sort of enterprise. I won't go to bed; that is too base.

Let me see if I can't nail that idea. It was about getting an unfavorable opinion—no, not that, but about putting my case in the hands of a just enemy; I can't think what my case was; and the enemy seemed to play me false—came round to my side. How curious! I can't get any nearer it than that. I have the strangest indifference about it all, and perhaps that is why I can't express it. One torment drives another out. I suppose hell is having no change of subject; the damnable iteration makes the hellishness. In the last week I have known what this infernal monotony was; but I can't remember what it was about.

I am going to keep writing away. If I pull through, I can make copy of it; if I don't, you can.

What a disgusting pose! But there is an awful reality in it, too. I am going to reach that before I quit, and then I shall stop, and carry this out and mail it. There is a postal box just round the corner; my legs ought to do that much for me. I must keep on foot till morning, and then get an ambulance and go to some hospital; I won't be sick on their hands, here; that would be too —

I should like to be at home, in Timber Creek. I used to hate it because it was like a prison, and I wanted to escape. Wottoma seemed a metropolis; but you must come to New York if you want to see what a metropolis is. I haven't begun my epic yet. I haven't written to my mother, for more than a week. I hate to write, for I don't like her knowing that I have the grippe. I wish you —.

Don't exploit me in the *Day* till I want the facts to come out. Perhaps — I shall have to stop, my head hurts so —

XXXVII

From MISS FRANCES DENNAM *to* MRS. DENNAM,
Lake Ridge.

NEW YORK, *February 15, 1902.*

Dear Mother:

Last night, I told you that I had pulled up my
principles by the roots, and thrown them out on the
woodpile in the backyard, and to-night I have to in-
form you that Miss Ralson has cast her proprieties to
the four winds, and we are both luxuriating in a
freedom from moral restraint which I don't see any
end to.

She came in a few minutes after Mr. Ardith left,
yesterday, and when I told her that he had been
there she was so angry with me for not keeping him
that I did not know but she was going to hit me.
She did manage to control herself long enough to let
me explain that he had come to see me and not her,

but not much longer. I had to tell her what he had said, and then I never saw such a passion as she flew out in. She wanted to know why Mr. Ardith should make a confidant of *me*, and appeal to me for my opinion in a matter that did not concern me; and when I made her realize that I had not asked for his confidence, and I had not given him any opinion, she was more furious than ever, and accused me of unjustly blaming him. She said she supposed I sided with those miserable Baysleys, because they were poor, and that she always knew I hated her. But she did not care, and if the whole Baysley family was at the point of death, it would not make the least difference to her. She said that she had seen from the first that I disliked Mr. Ardith as much as I did her, and that I had jumped at the chance to make him believe he had been doing wrong.

I can stand a good deal, and I had excused her unreasonableness to her unhappiness, but when it came to that, *I* flew out, too. Or rather, I flew *in*, for you know that when I am mad I do not say much about it. I suppose I got a little white, (whity-brown would suit my complexion better) for she looked scared; and when I went for my jacket and hat and started toward the door, without saying a single word, she began trying to make some sort of apology. She was so incoherent, that if I had not been mad through and through I should have wanted to laugh, and I did pity her enough to cry. She followed me into the vestibule, and asked me what I was doing, and where I was going; and when I would not answer, she called after me, " *Go*, then! " and burst out sobbing.

But I shut myself out, and I did not have a very good night. The fact is, I do love that family, if they *are* rich; and my heart ached for the poor soul, though she had said such insulting things that I could not bear it. Still, I knew I ought to have considered that as she could not hurt Mr. Ardith for the mischief he had made, she had to hurt me. I took it out of him for the mischief he had made in some one-sided dialogues of the sort we hold with people we are excited about, and they have not a word to say for themselves, and I made up for my mealy-mouthedness with him in the afternoon. I spoke daggers, I can tell you, but I retracted every single dagger when Miss Ralson came up in her automobile this morning to get me to go over to the Baysleys' with her. Old Mr. Baysley had just been at the Walhondia to say that Mr. Ardith was down with the grippe, the worst way, and that he was out of his head, and they did not know what to do. He seemed to have been up all night, when Mr. Baysley found him in his room at breakfast time, and he had a letter before him on the table, and was trying to write. They got a doctor who found Mr. Ardith in a high fever, and got him to bed somehow; and Mr. Baysley seemed to have left pretty much the whole family watching with him, while he came to tell the Ralsons. Mr. Ralson is away at Washington, but America saw Mr. Baysley, and she telephoned their own doctor to send a trained nurse to the Baysleys' instantly, and we found the nurse there taking possession when we arrived.

America wanted to go right in to see Mr. Ardith, but the nurse said she had better not, and we had to stay in the parlor at the other end of the flat, and hear his crazy talk coming through the corrider. The nurse would not say whether he was very bad or not, she said the case was one of the sudden kind, when the patients are delirious, and that she would rather we would talk with the doctor about it. She was so non-committal that it seemed to me as if I had never held my tongue in my life, and she scared us a great deal worse than if she had told us he was dying.

You remember how it was at Lake Ridge, when everybody had the grippe; some of them tried to kill themselves, and I guess Mr. Ardith is almost like that. The nurse would not stay with us a moment, hardly, but went right back to him, and shut his room door; she seemed to think he ought to have two nurses; but what they would do in that little bit of a flat I don't see.

While we sat there waiting for the Ralsons' doctor to come, (America had asked him to, when she telephoned for the nurse,) the youngest Baysley girl came in with the unfinished letter that they had found Mr. Ardith writing at in the morning, and gave it to Miss Ralson. She looked awfully pale, and so weak she could hardly put one foot before the other, and I fairly hated America Ralson. But I know there was no sense in that, for if he did not care for the girl— Oh, I have got so mixed up, I don't know what to think, and sometimes I feel as if there was no way to settle it but for Mr. Ardith— But *that* wouldn't settle the eternal right and wrong of it, either. The wretched child coughed so when she tried to speak to America, that she could not really say anything coherent, and she handed America the letter without explaining, and went out of the room without hardly looking at us; but I knew what was in her heart.

Nobody could have explained the letter: it was a crazy whirl of words, almost from the beginning, and at the end it went off into mere scribble. But we made out that why they wanted us to see it was that in one place he spoke of his mother, and wished he was at home. The letter was to some friend of his in the Iowa town where the Ralsons used to live, and America said she knew where his mother lived, and she would telegraph her at once. She had been perfectly cowed ever since she came into the apartment, and the Baysley girl's bringing her the letter, and making her feel how she hated her had been the last touch. But as soon as she could find something to do, she braced right up, and it didn't make any difference whether it was the wrong thing. I had the greatest time to get her to wait till she had seen her own doctor and got his opinion of Mr. Ardith before she went out to telegraph his mother; but I did manage it, and when the doctor came at last, I persuaded her to let me speak with him first.

It was a good thing I did, and got him to modify what he said, for he told me it was the worst kind of an attack, and there were nine chances out of ten

against Mr. Ardith. He said it was useless to telegraph his mother, at least till later in the day, for if
he did not improve she could not get here in time,
and if he did, we could send some encouraging
message. I prepared him for America, with some
hint of how the land lay, so that when he came in to
see her, he fibbed nobly. He said there was absolutely nothing we could do there, and we had better
go away. He promised to stay himself, and laughed
at her anxiety. The nurse was the very best on his
list, and besides—here he made his little break—the
people of the house seemed to be devotedly attached
to the young man, and would give any help that the
nurse could need. We could come again when his
fever had been subdued, but until it was, it would be
worse than useless for his friends to see him. We
could do no good; we could only do harm.

I could see America wince when he praised the
devotion of the Baysleys, and I knew what a pang it
was for her to think that other girl could be there
with him and do things for him, and she could not.
Don't you think it was rather cruel yourself, mother?
I changed all round, anyway, and pitied her as much
as 1 had pitied the Baysley girl before; for whatever
Mr. Ardith has done, America Ralson has done

nothing wrong. She has as good a right to care for him as if there were no other girl in the world, and she hasn't done the Baysley girl any more harm than the Baysley girl has done her. In fact they are both of them perfectly guiltless toward each other. It has taken me a good while to reason this out, but now I have got hold of the truth of the matter, I am going to hang on to it whether Mr. Ardith lives or dies. His living or dying has got nothing to do with the justice of the case; and the only thing that troubles me now is that those two innocent creatures should have such hate for each other in their hearts on his account. But that is perfectly inevitable, and I suppose that women will go on hating each other as they do as long as there is a man left to make trouble between them. When I realize that, I could almost wish there were no men, and I have to remember father, and what an angel he was, before I can reconcile myself. I do not know that men are so much to blame; they are just weak, and pulled about this way and that wherever they see a pretty face. Perhaps there ought not to be any pretty faces; if we were all plain, like me, I dare say the men would be all right. Not that I think Mr. Ardith has meant to do wrong: I want to keep that in mind, while I realize that Miss

Ralson is as good as the Baysley girl, and that just
now she is not as happy, and not as fortunate, with
all the money of the Cheese and Churn Trust behind
her.

I am writing this at the hotel, and America is in
her room writing a letter to Mr. Ardith's mother, to
be sent as soon as the doctor says she can be told of
his sickness.   Every now and then she runs in to ask
me whether she had better say this or that, or leave
so and so out.   My heart aches for her; but when
she puts her tragedy face in to ask whether I spell
grippe with one *p* and a final *e*, I want to laugh.

> Your affectionate daughter,
> FRANCES.

XXXVIII.

From Miss America Ralson *to* Mrs. Rebecca Ardith,
Timber Creek, Iowa.

The Walhondia, New York, *February the Fifteenth,
Nineteen Hundred and Two.*

Dear Mrs. Ardith:

I hope you will not be alarmed at getting this letter from a total stranger to you personally; though you may have heard your son speak of our family in Wottoma. The doctor wishes me to tell you that he is recovering from a pretty severe attack of the grippe, and will be about again in a few days. He is in good hands, and is having the best of medical care, and a trained nurse; so that you need feel no anxiety. The doctor did not want me to write to you, but I thought that if there was an interruption of his letters you would be uneasy, and I shall send this without consulting him, and keep you posted right along.

I do not know whether Mr. Ardith has told you

how much he has let us see him this winter. It has been very pleasant for us, especially for my mother, who enjoys talking with him about Wottoma; and my father thinks there is no one like him. He is away from home, at Washington, just now, or he would join my mother and myself in best regards.

Yours sincerely,

AMERICA RALSON.

P. S. I will write again to-morrow, and let you know how Mr. Ardith is. I suppose he has told you that he has rooms with a family from your place. They are very good people, and have every reason to be kind to him, for he helped them in their own sickness, and I am afraid he has taken the disease from them. But that is not their fault, though I think that as soon as he can be moved, he ought to be in more comfortable quarters. I do not mean that his present room is uncomfortable. It is at the back, and has the sun, and it is very quiet, but the flat is small, and they are a good deal crowded, especially as some of them are not quite well themselves yet.

XXXIX.

From Miss Frances Dennam *to* Mrs. Dennam,
Lake Ridge.

New York, *February 19, 1902.*

Dear Mother :

I have been so busy, the last three or four days,
flying back and forth between the Ralsons and the
Baysleys, that I have scarcely had time to write; and
as I had nothing decided to write about Mr. Ardith,
I thought I would wait. I knew, from your answer
to my last, how much you were interested, and now I
am glad to report that he is so much better as to be
almost out of danger. There is always danger that
pneumonia may set in, the doctor says, but as yet it
has not. Day before yesterday they nearly lost hope,
and when I found it out, I just wouldn't hold in any
longer. America was fairly frantic about him, in
spite of the lies we had kept telling her, but when I
told her the truth, it steadied her in the most wonder-

ful way. She insisted on going up and staying under the same roof with him, and helping do what could be done for him outside of his room. Her idea seemed to be to do as much for him as any of the Baysleys were doing, and not to let that other girl have it to say or to think that she had failed in anything; which was perfectly natural. But really there was nothing that either of them could do. In fact it needed a man, and the doctor substituted a man nurse for the woman. Mr. Ardith was so delirious at one time that he had to be held, to keep him from getting out of the window. But now he is in his right mind, and they are not afraid of anything but pneumonia.

I have had to stay here most of the time with Mrs. Ralson, and I have slept here the whole week. Mr. Ralson is still at Washington. There is some trouble about the Trust, and he is there on that account; I guess he is afraid of the government prosecuting him, or something of that kind; I don't know exactly. At any rate there he is, and we don't know just when he will be back.

FRANCES.

P. S. Miss Ralson had put a postscript to her letter to Mrs. Ardith, kind of blaming the Baysleys for

Mr. Ardith's having got the grippe from them; but I persuaded her to leave it out, and write her letter over. It was just as well, for it seems that Mrs. Ardith is having some trouble with her eyes, and had to take the letter to Mr. Baysley's brother, who is a minister out there, to have it read. He answered it for her and I don't know what he would have thought if he had had to answer that postscript. But now, that many of the pieces have been saved.

XL.

New York, *February 20, 1902.*

Dear Mother:

All continues to go well with Mr. Ardith, who isn't exactly bounding about yet, but is not so much in danger of pneumonia as the doctor thought. At any rate, Miss Ralson has felt it safe to come back here for the night, and I have got her in her room, making her write to her father, and tell him of her engagement. They take each other so casually that she thought it would be just as well if she waited till he got home. But I sat down on that good and hard, and she has listened to reason. She is not always as biddable as I should like, and I have just found out, by a letter that came from Timber Creek to-day, that she has not kept a pro ise she made me not to write anything to Mrs. Ardith without showing it to me. I

229

do not blame her altogether, for when she found that Mr. Ardith was in danger, she felt the responsibility of not writing so awfully that she wrote, and told his mother the truth.

The letter that came back was not from her, but from that Rev. Mr. Baysley again. He said that at first he had hesitated about reading Miss Ralson's letter to Mrs. Ardith, because she had not only the eye-trouble which prevented her from reading it herself, but was otherwise not able to take the journey to New York. Finally, he had decided to read it to her, and he said that he was glad, for she had taken it just as he could have wished. She sent messages to her son, to be given him as soon as he was in his right mind, telling him that she knew he would have patience with her not coming, and for him not to worry about her, for she would have courage for him. I thought when I was reading this word from her that if he was the kind of son that such a kind of mother could talk so to, he could not have acted heartlessly with that poor Baysley girl, and I have felt better about him than I did before.

But, mother, I wonder why people do not always come out with the whole truth at once when there is any kind of trouble or danger. The first thing when we knew that Mr. Ardith was very sick, we wanted to keep it from one another, but as soon as we owned the facts, Miss Ralson took courage from the instant she ought to have despaired, and when she told his mother how bad he was, his mother faced the chance of never seeing him again as bravely as if she could have come on here and saved him. I hope that if there is ever anything seriously the matter with you or Lizzie, you won't spare me a moment, to see how the cat is going to jump; and if I get the grippe, I promise to let you hear of my very worst symptoms from the start.

I only wish I could tell you what a nice, dignified letter that Mr. Baysley wrote to America for Mr. Ardith's mother. He is nothing but a poor country Baptist minister, and probably gets about five hundred dollars a year, and preaches the dullest kind of sermons. But when it came to being a ministering angel, he was there with the goods, as America would say; and I just know how he must have talked to that poor mother, and cheered her up. There wasn't anything pious in his letter; it was humble Christianity all through, and it was so delicate and refined in feeling. You lose your bearings a good deal in New York, with the talk about classes, upper and lower and middle, and in some of the newspapers that try to be "smart" you read things about common Americans that make your blood boil, if you haven't lost your bearings. But a letter like that country minister's out there in Iowa, makes me glad that I am a common American, and I believe the commoner we are the better we are. Those other Baysleys are as common as they can be, but they have behaved like saints; perhaps the saints are common; and what makes me love these Ralsons is that they are just as common as the Baysleys, in spite of their money, and always will be whether they get into the Four Hundred or not. May be the Four Hundred themselves would be common if you boiled them down. But that doesn't personally matter so much any more, for I don't believe Miss Ralson—

She has just been in here to show me her letter to her father, and she has come very near making me change my mind about her. We decided on some changes in the letter and then we sat talking, and suddenly she came out with something that happened the other night at the Baysleys'. She was sitting up after the family had gone to bed, in hopes that she might be asked to do something for Mr. Ardith and when she heard his muffled raving from the other end of the flat, she could not bear it, and crept down the corridor to his room, to try and make out what he was saying. The light in the corridor had been turned out, and it was so dark that she had to feel her way to the door, but she found it, and crouched on the floor there. She heard her own name, and Essie Baysley's, and he seemed to be talking to that friend of his in Wottoma that he was writing to when he was taken sick; but it was just a jumble of repetitions, and she could not make anything out of it. She was so anxious and absorbed that she did not notice at first something like some one catching their breath, very near her in the dark, but it must have come louder; and then she put out her hand. "And what do you think it was?" she fairly hissed out. "It was that Baysley girl! I felt as if I had touched a snake. *She was there listening!*"

She seemed to expect that I would be horrified and disgusted, but at first I could hardly help thinking that she must be joking. When I realized that she was not, I just hopped on her. "Why, what in the world were *you* doing? Hadn't *she* as much right to listen as *you* had? If that poor thing had left her own sick-bed, to come and hear his ravings, in the hopes of hearing something that would give her a little comfort or a little strength to bear her disappointment, I don't see why you should call her a snake for it. She was no more snake than you were, and there is just one thing that keeps me from hating you, and that is that you've been up so much, and are so crazy for want of sleep that you don't know what you're saying. " I gave it to her good and hot, and she seemed perfectly dumbfounded. She turned white, and then red, and then she burst out, " I will never speak to you again ! " and flung into her own room, and slammed the door after her.

I thought I knew just how much that meant, and I did not have to wait a great while, hearing her sob inside there, before she flung back again, and came and threw herself on her knees, and clutched me round the waist, and pulled me down to her. " I *am* crazy, and I don't know what I'm saying ! There ! " she shouted, and she looked so much like a big, unhappy child, that I could not help bending over and kissing her, though you know I am not much on the kiss. She begged my pardon, and I said she had not done *me* any harm, and then she wanted to know what she should do to make that Baysley girl forgive her, and I tried to find out whether she had said anything to the poor child or not. She was so ashamed that she would hardly confess, but it came out that she had said, " What are you eavesdropping here, for?" and the girl had burst out crying, and broken away from her, and run back to her room; and that was all.

You will think it was quite enough, and so do I; but what would you have advised Miss Ralson to do? She wanted to know whether she ought not to give Mr. Ardith up to that girl as soon as he was well enough for the sacrifice; but it seemed to me that this was the very last thing she ought to do, and that was what I said. I told her that it was for Mr. Ardith to give himself, or keep himself, and that her being willing to part with him had nothing to do with the rights and wrongs of the case. I talked her quiet at last, and she decided that all she could do was to beg the girl's pardon, and confess that she was sorry and ashamed. She has gone off to try and get some sleep, and in the morning she is going up to the Baysley's to offer reparation. The good thing about her is that she can feel for that child, and that if she could, she would hate herself because he likes her the best. But is there any real harm in his doing that? He is cruelly to blame for letting that poor thing care for him, and yet perhaps he could not have prevented it, and he may have been very much tempted. I have never seen the girl yet that could make *me* lose my head, but I see more and more that men are different. You ought to be glad that I am not

Your affectionate son,

FRANCES.

XLI.

From Mr. Otis Binning *to* Mrs. Walter Binning,
Boston.

New York, *February 23, 1902.*

Dear Margaret:

The Prince of Prussia has gone off to the West,
and given us a little breathing-space, and I am able
to detach my thoughts from him, and devote them to
this sort of one-sided communion with you. Do you
know, I am becoming really fond of it, and should
miss it if you happened to telegraph me some fine
day that you were rather tired of my letters? I
haven't written such long ones since my first year at
Harvard, when I "corresponded" with a young lady
of this city, about whom I was just then very much
in earnest. I have not the least notion what became
of her, except that she married some one beside myself, and is perhaps no longer extant. I do not account

for this conjecture except from the feeling that it is graceful and becoming for our first loves to die; I should hate meeting mine, in this world, of all things.

The literary superstition concerning us elderly fellows is (or used to be in the good old Thackeray times,) that we are always thinking of our first loves, and are going about rather droopingly on account of them. My own experience is that we are doing nothing of the kind. We are the only cheerful people in the world, and so long as we keep single, we are impartially impassioned of almost every interesting type of woman that we meet. I find the greatest pleasure in bestowing my affections right and left, and I enjoy a delightful surprise in finding them hold out in spite of my lavish use of them. If I totted up the number of my loves, young and old, since I came here early in December, Leperello's list would be nothing to it. And they are such innocent infatuations! As you must own, they certainly do not interfere with my devotion to you, in that friendship which constitutes us the mirror of brothers-and-sisters-in-law, and I know you will not mind my being very much absorbed just now in Miss Ralson's secretary. In fact, the absorption is quite in your interest, and involves the hope of surprising some further facts of the little romance in which I seem to have interested you so much beyond its merits or mine.

I do not know why I should have fancied, after I parted with my young Mr. Ardith the last time I saw him in the Park, that he might apply my counsel to an interview with Miss Dennam, on his way home to begin having the grippe. He has been having it ever since, in a form that at first alarmed his friends for him, though now he is out of danger. I understand, by no means so fully as I should like, that the glowing daughter of the Trust has seen that he wanted for nothing, in his sufferings, and I have found her away from home in both of the calls I have made at the Walhondia. Whether she was beside his couch or not, on these occasions, I cannot say, but for the sake of the old-fashioned fiction in which the heroines were always nursing their loves through critical sicknesses, let us hope so, Margaret. Her getting the grippe herself is something we would gladly have allowed in such a case.

Her absence has left me the freer opportunity for the employment of any subtlety I may possess in the study of her lieutenant, in whom I have joyfully divined a belated and dislocated Puritan. It has been very interesting to find what we call the New England conscience coming from Western New York, but that anxious and righteous spirit is always in the world, and owns no time or clime exclusively. The sense of personal responsibility for evil in one's self and in others is as rife in every religion—and irreligion for that matter—as it was in Massachusetts Bay in the seventeenth century, and I will confess a malign pleasure which I have taken in teasing it in Miss Dennam. To indulge this, I have gone so far as to tell her of my last meeting with young Ardith, and of his strange problem, and I have admired the struggle in her transparent soul with the question whether it was quite truthful to forbear owning that she knew of it already. It was a spectacle the more interesting because of the humor which qualified her scruple, and enabled her to experience the ordeal objectively, as it were. This gave it the quaintness, which is perhaps the note of her whole personality, and which I despair of making you feel.

Though she could not hide the fact, she did hide the correlated facts, and I can only surmise a tragedy lurking below her silence. I am afraid there is something worse than the grippe in Mr. Ardith's case. Just for the dramatic interest, wouldn't you like to imagine his playing some sort of double part, with that single selfishness which is the unique force of duplicity ? I hinted at some such mystery, but it was not intimated to me in return that I was right. It was there that my hermit thrush became a sphinx, and refused to read the riddle she had not asked. That is the reason I cannot be more explicit with you at present, and must leave you at such a poignant moment of the story, which I hope is to be continued. If you suffer, remember that I suffer with you.

Yours affectionately,

OTIS.

XLII.

From ABNER J. BAYSLEY *to* REV. WILLIAM BAYSLEY
Timber Creek.

N. Y. *Feb. 23, 1902.*

Dr Bro:

Yrs. of Friday to hand. Would say that young Ardith is out of danger. He ought to be, with the care he has had from all hands, including two doctors, man nurse and our whole family, up with him day and night most of the time. You can tell his mother not to worry; he is getting along first rate.

I guess from this out we can do any worrying ourselves that there is any call for. There has been pretty curious goings on here since that he took to his bed, and unless I am a good deal mistaken somebody has got to pay for it. Looks now, when he was fooling with Essie, like he had somebody else on the hook at the same time. I don't want to mention any names, yet, but you mustn't be surprised if some

242

things come out that wont show that fellow in the best of lights. I am not blaming anybody but him, and I hain't blamed *him* to his face, for he ain't strong enough to stand it. But if he thinks he can make a poor girl believe he's engaged to her, and at the same time get engaged to a rich girl, he is mistaken. That is about the way the land lays, and it don't seem to mother and I that it looks well for young A. I am not saying when we were all down with the grippe, here, but what he seemed to act the friend. He helped about the house like a good fellow, and when there was nobody around but Ess, he lent a hand at everything going. But the question is whether he done it for us, or done it for himself, or whether he was not just trying to have a good time as it went along.

Old Ralson's girl seems to think he belongs to her, somehow, and she has been here ordering round as if she owned things. Ess and her come into collision one night when they were both hanging round outside his door, and America Ralson said things to Ess that I wont let any one say to a daughter of mine, I don't care who she is, or what her father is. He may own the Cheese and Churn Trust, but he don't own me. We would not found out anything about it if mother had not heard Ess crying when she got back to her room, and went in and just made her say what the matter was. I tell you I feel pretty mad, and I am not going to let myself be imposed on if I *am* a Christian.

So I think you can let up a little on the consolation with Mrs. Ardith till we see how this thing is going to come out. He has got to do the right thing by Essie, or I will know the reason why. No more at present, but I thought I would just give you a hint.

Will write you again when I have had my talk with Ardith. With our united love to your family,

Yr aff. bro.

ABNER.

XLIII

From Mrs. Abner J. Baysley, *to* Mrs. Wm. Baysley,
Timber Creek.

New York, *February 24, 1902.*

Dear Sister:

Father has sent off a letter to William that I do not know as I feel exactly right about. You know how all up or all down he is, and he never sees anything but what is either black as night or bright as the noonday. I have talked with Essie more than he has, and I know the rights of the case a good deal better. I put the blame, what there is, on Mr. Ardith; and yet I do not know as he meant any harm. It was wrong for him to fool with Essie, if he was honestly in love with some one else, but then I cannot say that it was anything more than fooling on his part. I suppose it is what goes on with young people most of the while, and though I never liked it, and do not approve of such things, I am not going to pretend that it was not the same with me in my young days, or you either. The children are as good girls as ever stepped, and just as particular; but I am not going to say they have never let fellows kiss them without meaning anything by it. I hear it is not so much the custom in the city, any more; but you and I both know that it is different in the country. Besides Essie was only sixteen last November, and he might have looked upon her as a child; he is ten years older. When the rest of us were sick, and he was helping her about the work that there was nobody but her to do, and he saw her so anxious and distracted, it was natural for him to try to comfort her; and you know how our feelings are mixed up at that age, so that we can hardly tell one from the other. One thing is certain: he never asked her to be engaged to him, and I am not going to have him treated as if he had broken a promise to her, in getting engaged to anybody else. It is very hard for her, and she feels it; but if we go back to bygones, it was our fault ever having him come here. Before father got his increase of salary, (and it was Mr. Ardith that got it for him,) we were so hard put to it to make both ends meet here, where everything is so high, that we fairly made a set at him to take our spare room. I am ashamed to think of it now, and so I tell father when he wants to bring him to book, as he calls it. I just know that he took the room out of the kindness of his heart, and he has been like a son and a brother to the whole family ever since. Any girl might be glad to get him, but I would not have a girl of mine try to get him, for the world, unless he wanted her. That is the way I feel about it; and Emmeline, I am not going to let my judgment be clouded. He is a good young man, I don't care what they say, and all during his delirium he kept raving and explaining, first to one and then to another, that he was not engaged to Essie, and never had been, but he did like her, though not in that way exactly; or so much. I believe he has tried to be honest, and that he has suffered more than any one else, from letting his foolishness overcome him. Essie has got to stand it. She was not to blame, for she did not know that she was getting so attached to him; but I guess she is not so attached but what she can get over it.

You may think this is rather of an unnatural way for a mother to talk, but the way I look at it is that a mother can love her children all she need to, and still not be a fool about them, and I believe that is the way William will look at it too.

With love,

JANE BAYSLEY.

XLIV.

From Miss Frances Dennam *to* Mrs. Dennam,
Lake Ridge.

New York, *March 4, 1902.*

Dear Mother :

I must say you do not seem very grateful for the letters that I have written to keep you and Lizzie along, you romantic things, while there has been nothing decisive happening here. You talk as if I had not told you anything worth knowing since my voluminous effort of February 20th. What did you expect, I wonder ? Did you suppose I was writing a story, and could make up a chapter whenever I chose ? Well, I almost wish I had done it, and stuffed you full of fibs. It would have been pleasanter than giving you the cold facts, now that something *has* happened, at last.

Mr. Ardith has just been here looking so sick, so

sick, and coughing to break anybody's heart. It is the first time he has been out since he was taken down three weeks ago, and I don't believe the doctor knew he was coming now. I have been spending the nights at home, lately, and I could hardly recognize his voice, when I heard him talking, after the maid let me in, from where I stopped in the vestibule. He spoke so weakly and huskily, and every now and then he broke down coughing, and now and then laughing so sadly it made my flesh creep. The parlor of the apartment is between the vestibule and the little room that belongs to me, when I am here, and where I always write Miss Ralson's letters; but a door opens from the vestibule into Mrs. Ralson's room, and I decided to go there, when America seemed to hear me, and called out, "Come in here, Miss Dennam! Mr. Ardith is here. Come and hear what he is saying!"

Her voice sounded quite wild, and I hesitated, but before I could escape into her mother's room she came running out, and pulled me in, like a crazy thing. Her face was drenched with crying, and there stood Mr. Ardith holding himself up by the table, and pale as death, trying to smile, when he put out his hand to me. She did not notice his gesture, but pushed me into a chair on the other side of the room and said, "Sit down, sit down, Mr. Ardith, and let Miss Dennam hear what you have been saying. I want her to be judge between us."

She took a big chair herself, and leaned forward with her elbow on one of the arms, and her chin in her hand, with a mocking expression of attention. He sank into the chair behind him, not as if he wished to, but as if he were not able to keep on foot any longer, and she went on: "Come, begin! I have forgotten a good deal of what you said, and it will all be fresh to Miss Dennam." I began, "Miss Ralson, I am going to your mother," and I got up, but she ran and pushed me down again, and then took the same attitude as before in her own chair, and waited for him to speak. He only hung his head, with a pitiful, sidelong glance at me. "What! you are not going on?" she said. "Well, then, I will tell Miss Dennam, myself. Part of it is rather ancient history, but she wont mind hearing it once more." Then she turned to me, "Mr. Ardith has just driven down to the Walhondia from his apartments on the West Side to announce the end of our engagement."

You will say that I ought to have boxed her ears, and I felt like it; but I have not lived with her two months without understanding that a brutal speech like that was only the expression of suffering that could not relieve itself any other way. I hated her for it, but I pitied her too. Besides, it was not my business to box her ears, and the most I could do was to make another start for the door. This time it was Mr. Ardith who stopped me. "Don't go," he said hoarsely. "Let America tell you." "Yes, let me give you his reasons; he has reasons!" she broke in, but without noticing her, he went on, to me: "I came to you once before for your judgment."

She did not seem to take that in, or else she was too preoccupied with what was in her mind. "Yes, indeed, he has reasons, and you will be surprised how good they are. He has found out—with the help of the Baysley family, of course—that he has been making love to that girl, up there, without realizing it, and that he has got her so much in love with him that it will kill her if he breaks with her. He says that he does not really care for her, and that he does not expect to be happy with her. His idea is that I have everything in the world to make me happy, and that I will not mind giving up a mere trifle like him to a poor girl who wants him so much worse." That was frightfully vulgar, mother; but I am beginning to find out that real feeling is *always* vulgar; and I knew that

if a girl like America Ralson would let herself say
such things it must be because her soul was almost
torn with red-hot pincers. She whirled her face round
from me to him: "Is that it? Have I understated
it, or overstated it?" "No," he said, "you have
stated it," and she turned back to me again, "Well,
and what do you think of it?"

Then I broke out. "I don't think anything about
it, and I wont. You had no right to make me come
in here. If you didn't care for me, you ought to care
for him." "I intend to care for myself," she said.
"He has been telling me that he cares the whole
world for me, and no matter how much I care for him
I must give him up to somebody he doesn't care for
at all. He can't say why it would be better for me to
suffer than for her. He has given me his word, and
he hasn't given her his word; perhaps that's why he
can take it back from me, and can't from her." I
knew she was just saying that to hurt him, and she
wished to hurt him because she worshipped him; but
it seemed to me that she was talking sense, too,
though I don't believe she knew it. He must have
felt something like that too, for he got up and steadied
himself on his feet without the help of the table, and
said, "I don't take it back, and I wont. My love is

yours, and my life." It sounds rather silly, when
you write such speeches, back and forth, but the poor
things were in dead earnest, when they made them,
and so was I when I heard them. I looked at America,
for what she would do next, and I was ready to fly
out of the room at short notice.

She had got up, too, and she said scornfully, "Oh,
you've convinced me! I don't want your love now,
or your life." He looked at her like death. "You
mustn't let me keep you, Mr. Ardith, from—your
friends. Good-bye." She held out her hand to him,
but he did not offer to take it. He just kept looking
at her, and then he turned away to the door. But
she wailed after him in the greatest astonishment,
"Why, are you *going?*" and he turned, and she held
her arms toward him. I knew that this was the time
for me to fly out of the room and I flew. With the
door between them and me, I tried to collect my
thoughts, as people used to do in the novels, but the
most that I could scrape together was that they were
acting sensibly, at last, if they *were* acting selfishly,
and their love was keeping them from behaving falsely,
no matter how cruelly he would have to behave to
that other girl. Mother, I never had such hard work
in the world to keep from listening at a keyhole as I

did then, and I hope some day I shall be rewarded. You may be surprised, but I was so honorable that I went and raised the window, at the risk of taking my death of cold, and let the roar of the Avenue come in so that I could not hear anything through the door. I was determined to freeze rather than eavesdrop, and I had left my wraps in the vestibule. I could not get to Mrs. Ralson's room without going back through the parlor, and I was in for it as long as they chose to keep me there. From the indications, I expected that they might keep me the whole forenoon, and I was composing a few last dying messages to you and Lizzie, when the door opened, and Miss Ralson came in.

"Well," she said, calmly, "it's over." "Over?" I gasped back at her. "You don't mean that"— "We've given each other up! That's what we've done. He's gone back to her." Before I could stop myself I had said, "What fools!" and she did not give me time to take it back. "Oh, fools, yes! What else did you expect?" and I came back with as much of an answer as she would let me: "I thought you were making up, and—" "Did you suppose I could let him go against his conscience?" She sank down in an armchair, looking somehow shrunken and little, like the same person wrung out, if you can understand,

and the sight of her, and the knowledge of what she must have been through, for a girl like her to come to that, made me furious.

"Why shouldn't he have *you* on his conscience as well as her?" I said, but she only shook her head, and sort of sighed. "That is different. He was right. But if he was wrong, I had to give him up, just the same."

Do you think she had, mother? And what does Lizzie think?

I can't stand it anyhow; I know it can't be right. That child has just set her heart on him because he has been good to her, and she would be over it in a few months; but America is a woman; she is twenty-five years old; as old as he is, nearly; and it is a serious thing with her; it is a matter of life and death.

It is none of my business, but I cannot let it go so. I feel like going up there to the Baysleys' and having it out with them myself, and telling them what a pack of simpletons they are, and how they are just making misery for themselves, as well as everybody else.

But of course, that wouldn't do. Thank goodness, Mr. Ralson is coming home to-night, and if there is the slightest opening, I think I can get in some good work with him. Anyway I have got my war-paint on, and I am not going to bury the hatchet in a hurry, I can tell you.

Your affectionate daughter,

BLOOD-IN-THE-EYES DENNAM.

XLV.

From WALLACE ARDITH *to* A. L. WIBBERT, *Wottoma.*
NEW YORK, *March 4, 1902.*

My dear Lincoln:

I have been down, and nearly under, with the grippe, but am up at last, and it might have been better if I were not. Death would have been much simpler than life, for me.

I hope you will not be hurt at my asking you to send me back my letters. I have had my parting with A. R., preparatory to my meeting with E. B., and it seems right that I should destroy all written records of the past that relate to A. R. I have come back to this hotel, and you can send them here. I could not stay any longer at the B.s' under the circumstances, but I shall go round there to-night and try to do what is right.

But what is right? Was breaking with A. R., right when I love her with my whole heart and soul, and is

257

it right to make good to E. B. the things that she took for granted? Both of these alternatives are utterly false, and yet they seem my duty. Why? I know no other reason than because I wish to do neither, and that there is no other way to punish myself for what I have done. It is illogical and unreasonable, of course, but there seems nothing else.

I have not the strength to write more, at present. You can know the situation from what I have told you before; but if not, I cannot help it. I will write again as soon as there is something more. Send this letter back with the others, and I will feel that the incident is closed.

Yours faithfully,

W. ARDITH.

XLVI.

New York, *March 5, 1902.*

Dear Mother :

Yesterday was certainly a day of the craziest events that ever happened, and what to-day will be, goodness only knows. It has not had time to get in its work, yet, for it is only six o'clock in the morning, and I am scribbling this with a pencil in bed, to pass away the time till I can get up with the hope of something to eat : I am furiously hungry, and I have got to thinking, so I can't sleep any longer. The principals of the affair are slumbering peacefully, while I, an innocent second, have hardly had two consecutive winks the whole night.

After I sent off my massive missive to you yesterday, I had to lunch with Miss Ralson, who had such an appetite as I have never seen outside of a house

259

of mourning; the strongest emotions seem to leave one the hollowest. But I pitied her, and when she proposed going to a matinée, I perfectly understood her: she had got to kill time from this out, and she could not begin a moment too soon. And where do you think we decided to go? Well, to a sort of burlesque place, where there are three broken-English-speaking Germans that get you into perfect gales. I do not know how we came to think of it, but we did, both together; and I suppose it was because we thought something like that would help her to take her mind off itself better than anything else. Well, it did, almost from the first moment of the sort of comic opera, with dancing in it, that I should blush to have you see me see. Then came a parody of a play that is running at another theatre, and that was just as killing, without being as scandalous as the opera; I suppose because several women's part was taken by men: I don't know why the men are always more decent on the stage than the women are, even when the men are acting women.

It seemed to be an actressy sort of matinée; you could tell the strong professional faces, and the intense professional hats and gowns; and you could be perfectly safe that you would not see anybody you knew

in the whole crowd.   I do not believe America cared
what sort of crowd it was; what she wanted to do
was not to think; and as I only know about ten people in New York, I was not anxious.   But whom do
you think we saw coming out of the vestibule of the
theatre, a little ahead of us?   The psychological Mr.
Binning!   He had been there, too, and he was looking
at the photographs of the actresses on the easels in
the corridor, standing slanted over, with his cane
under his arm, and his silk-hatted head bent to one
side, critically.   Fortunately, he had his back to us,
and I clutched America by the arm, and dragged her
out, and never let her stop till we had mixed ourselves
up with the crowd coming out of one of the proper
theatres.   Then I slowed up and explained, and after
awhile Mr. Binning overtook us, and lifted his hat
and asked us if we were walking, and might he walk
with us as far as our hotel.

Of course, I shall never know whether he had seen
us coming out of that place, but he confessed that he
had been there himself, and said he had been immensely amused; it was so amusing that it was a pity
it was not more adapted to ladies, and we pretended
that we had hardly ever heard of it, and made him
explain a little, which he did very skillfully ; and then

we talked of the piece at the theatre we had seemed
to come out of ; we had fortunately seen it just before
Mr. Ardith was taken sick. If this was a little wicked,
and I do not say it was perfectly truthful, I excused
myself, because I could see that it was helping tide
America over. Mr. Binning had been so nice that we
asked him to come in and have tea with us, and you
would never have imagined that America had been
through anything half as bad as a hard day with the
dress-maker. But *I* should, and when I saw the ex-
haustion in her eyes, and heard it in her voice, I got
her away for an imaginary engagement, and made Mr.
Binning believe that I wanted him to stay on with me.
He seemed very glad to stay on with any one, and
took cup after cup of tea, enough to keep him awake
the whole night. He is a very sly old tommy, and I
think he smelt a mouse of some sort, for every now
and then he would come back from some other subject, and artfully bring the talk round to Mr. Ardith.
He pretended to be ever so much interested in him ;
he thinks, or says he thinks, he is very talented, and
that his greatest danger is getting himself involved in
some sort of love-affair, and spoiling his career with
some sort of disadvantageous early marriage. He was
really very subtle in the analysis he made of Mr.

Ardith's nature: he said he was the sort of person
to increase the danger of any situation he found himself in by fancying things far beyond the reality; that
he was capable of becoming anything he dreaded
becoming; he had a supersensitive conscience, and
would sacrifice himself or anybody else to its aberra-
tions. I could hardly believe he was not onto the
facts, especially when he asked where Mr. Ardith
lived, and who had taken care of him in his grippe.
When I told him, he asked if there were daughters,
and I said there were two. He said, "Ah!" as if
that told the whole story, and then he said "Which?"
so slyly that I wanted to get up and box his old ears.
He asked all sorts of questions about the Baysleys,
but I was a tabby, if he *was* a tommy, and he did not
know anything I did not want him to. Suddenly he
switched off to Miss Ralson, and asked if she were
not very romantic. I asked him why he thought so,
and he said, merely because she always seemed so
matter-of-fact; he had noticed that practical people
were always full of romantic potentialities. He began
to talk about her beauty; and it seemed to him that
she was built so generously, and he hoped that she
would not throw herself away at the first opportunity;
such a girl could make the right man supremely happy.

He suddenly asked when we expected Mr. Ralson back; he hoped he was not anxious about the Trust on account of the bluff the government was making; it was nothing but a bluff. Then, before I knew it, he was talking about Mr. Ardith again, and saying it was delightful to see two men of such different types as he and Mr. Ralson liking each other. Mr. Ralson was charmingly fond of the young fellow.

He had managed to make it so impersonal that I could not feel that it was impertinent. You might say it was patronizing, for he talked of the Ralsons and Mr. Ardith as if they were a different order of beings from himself. I was just getting ready to resent that when he asked Mr. Ardith's address, and said he was going to venture to call upon him; then he rose, with the ease of a person who has been used to managing such things all his life, and shook hands with me, and got himself away before I could say Jack Robinson.

You will infer from my beginning to use ink here that I am out of bed. I have had my coffee, but the others have not breakfasted yet, and I have the time and have got the strength to go on with this yarn for a while longer.

Mr. Ralson arrived from Washington on the 6.23, last night and it seemed to me that he was in the hotel almost before Mr. Binning was out of it, but there must have been an interval, for I was with Mrs. Ralson, comforting her against her fears of accidents to Mr. Ralson, and reassuring her about America and her headache, and proving to her that it was mathematically impossible for Mr. Ardith to have a relapse from having come out too soon, when Mr. Ralson arrived to relieve me. Then he and I had rather a difficult dinner together, for it is hard to eat in absolute silence even when you do not want to talk; but long before I was ready for the order, he had pushed back his plate (as I suppose he used to do when he ate his whole dinner off one plate,) and lit his cigar, with his chair tilted on its hind legs, and was saying " Now tell me about Make. "

I do not believe I could ever have done it, if I had not been like the beaver that clomb the tree, and had to. But I did do it, with no more interruption from Mr. Ralson than an occasional snort, and " Humph ! " and a question now and then to make me keep on. Things must have been going the way of the Trust at Washington, for he was in a very good humor, and when he began to speak, he took a very optimistic view of the matter. He just said, "I guess we can arrange that all right, if Ardith don't insist on making a fool of himself. We're a party in interest as much as the Baysleys, and I don't propose to let them walk over us if they *are* dependent on me for their living." That way of looking at the case seemed to amuse him, and he laughed. "Of course, I will do the fair thing by them," he said.

He had made me tell all I knew, and now he began to cross-question me; and I suppose I looked worried, for he apologized, "I have to make sure of my ground, you know," and then he went into a long revery, and smoked and smoked. Every now and then he seemed as if he were going to say something, but he only made a noise in his throat, and kept on smoking. I had not heard any ring, when the maid came in with the sort of card they give people to send up their names on from the office, and he said, "Heigh! What's this?" and looked at it, at arm's length, to make out the name, and then said, "Yes, certainly, have him up," and kept smoking, and frowning through his smoke, while I was on pins and needles, till I heard some one being let into the vestibule, and hesitating there, and Mr. Ralson roared out, "Come in here!"

I had never seen Mr. Baysley before, but somehow

I knew who it was the moment I set eyes on him; and mother, I am sorry to say I did not like his looks. My sympathies were naturally with him and against Mr. Ralson, for we belong to the poor side and not the rich, and I do think the Baysleys have had a good deal to bear. But it is no use to pretend that hard luck does not take the manhood out of a man; when he has an inferior part in life to play, he begins to look the part, and he looks the superior part when he has that to play. Mr. Ralson, with his cloud of white hair, and his red face crossed by his big white moustache, and his large stomach swelling out through his unbuttoned coat, was " all there " as he came forward with his napkin in his hand; and poor Mr. Baysley, in his shabby overcoat, with his silly Fedora hat in his hand, and his frightened eyes running from Mr. Ralson to me and back, seemed to have left the best of himself somewhere else. Mr. Ralson gave a roaring laugh and held out the hand that hadn't the napkin in it. " Well, old Battery A ! " he shouted out, and a pitiful kind of smile came into Mr. Baysley's face, as if he did not dare quite believe in the appearance of friendliness. " What can I do for *you?* Have some coffee? Sit down—pull up ! " and Mr. Ralson dragged him by the hand toward the table, and

said to me, "Miss Dennam, will you make that girl
fetch Mr. Baysley a cup? Do' know whether you
know Miss Dennam, Mr. Baysley. Take off your overcoat. Have a cigar? And tell her to put down the
Scotch, too. I'm just off the train, and Miss Dennam
and I have been having a bite here. Sorry my wife
and daughter are not very well. How are your family?" "Well sir, we have had a good deal of sickness
this winter." "That so? Well, I've been away—
but come to think, I *had* heard something about it.
Grippe?" "Yes, sir. We have all been down with
it, and Mr. Ardith has had it too." "Oh, yes! Yes,
yes!" "He's been out for the first time, to-day,
and—he hasn't got in yet, or hadn't when I left home,
and moth— Mrs. Baysley was feeling a little anxious.
And I thought I would run down, and inquire if you
had happened to see anything of him here."

Mr. Baysley seemed to have hard work to get that
out, and did not seem much relieved afterwards, but
Mr. Ralson broke the ash of his cigar off into his
saucer, and answered cosily, "Why, yes, Miss Dennam tells me he was here this afternoon—or morning,
was it?—but I haven't seen him myself. He's
probably met some friends— Sugar?" By this time
Mr. Baysley had his coffee, and Mr. Ralson pushed

the sugarbowl towards him; and offered him a lighted match for his cigar. "I like my tobacco along with my coffee." Mr. Baysley submissively lighted his cigar, and with that and the coffee, he began to look a little less daunted in Mr. Ralson's presence. " It seems like old times to be drinking coffee again with you, Baysley; we used to take it out of a tin cup, and we didn't exactly have loaf sugar in it; we had to get our tobacco across the lines, when there was a Johnny handy that wanted coffee." That made Mr. Baysley laugh, and show most of his upper teeth gone, and cough out through the smoke, " Gay times!" and wag his head with more courage. I could make out that they had been soldiers together, in the Civil War; and they went on talking, and getting friendlier. But that did not make me any happier, for I saw just as well that Mr. Ralson was *working* Mr. Baysley, and that the poor, weak old creature was flattered, and was like putty in his hands. I knew he had come to talk with Mr. Ralson about Mr. Ardith, and probably he had told his wife that he was not going to let the Ralsons walk over them; for if Mr. Ardith had not come back to them, yet, they might very well have supposed that he was not coming back at all, and the Ralsons knew it. That was what his first remark indicated, but Mr. Ralson had got him far beyond that. If he had met Mr. Baysley roughly, perhaps Mr. Baysley would have held his ground, but as it was he was not left a leg to stand on, whatever he thought his rights were. It made me fairly sick, and when Mr. Ralson said, "Why don't that girl bring the Scotch?" I could not stand it any longer. I got up and said I would send her with it, and I went in to Mrs. Ralson, and let her talk her nerves down, after I had made excuses for Miss Ralson's headache, and Mr. Ralson's business caller. She did not ask who it was with him; and after awhile she said she believed she would go to bed, and I came to my own room, and have been writing to you ever since.

It is ten o'clock, and I have just heard Mr. Ralson and Mr. Baysley coming out into the vestibule together, shouting and laughing. Mr. Baysley's voice was the same, but it was in quite another key, so I should have hardly known it, when I heard him saying, "Well, sir, you done the handsome thing, and I'll see that there's no trouble." "If it isn't right," I heard Mr. Ralson answer, "I'll *make* it right." "Oh, it's all right. It'll fix the old place up in good shape; and if you make the salary the same in Timber Creek

as what it is here"— "Sure!" "Then we don't
need to say anything more about it. Well, sir, good-
night—Jim." "Good night, Ab." "He, he!"
"Haw, haw!"

I feel as if I had overheard something awful, and
the cold chills are running down my back; but I do
not know any more than you do what those two miserable men meant, and I leave you to find out for
yourselves. *I* am going to bed.

I seem to be keeping a diary instead of writing a
letter. I began this quite gaily on the 5th, expecting
to mail it that day, and here I am dragging on through
the 7th, and not seeing the end yet. Well, one thing:
I will never keep another diary.

To my great surprise I did get to sleep towards
morning, but a little after eight I was roused from my
wicked dreams by the maid, who came to tell me that
there was a lady in the vestibule wanting to see Mr.
Ralson, and that she was afraid to call him, and what
should she do? Of course I asked, "What kind of
lady?" and what her name was, but the maid did not
know, and my mind worked round from female
anarchists to destitute females, and then I decided
to get up and go see for myself, and get rid of

the lady, who was unseasonable, whatever she was.

I was rewarded by finding Mrs. Baysley, who accounted for her getting into the apartment at that hour by saying that she had come directly up in the elevator to the number that her husband had given her. She was only anxious apparently to make sure that Mr. Ralson had not gone out, and said she was not in a hurry, but could wait till he had his breakfast, if he could not see her before. I made her come into the parlor, and asked her to share my coffee, but she said she had been to breakfast, and did not want anything more at present. I tried to talk with her, but her mind seemed so centered on something, that I could not get more than a word at a time out of her, and she would not give me any clew to what she wanted. She just sat there drooping in her chair, and holding something in her folded hands that was like a scrap of paper; and I decided that if Mr. Ralson kept her waiting a great while, I would go and knock on his door myself, and take the consequences, when America came into the room.

I did not know she was up, and it startled me, but I could not help noticing how fresh and strong and beautiful she looked. If she had shared my vigils, she did not show it, and Mrs. Baysley seemed to wither before her, as Mr. Baysley had withered before her father. She swept by her without seeing her, and said to me, "I wish you would give me some of your coffee, Miss Dennam; I'm half-starved," and I had to say, "Mrs. Baysley is here," before she noticed her. She gave a start, at the name, and as she whirled round, and looked at her, I could see the disgust come into her face. Mrs. Baysley stood up in front of her chair without offering to come forward, and for a dreadful moment America did not move, either. Then she went to her, and put out her hand. "Wont you have some breakfast, Mrs. Baysley?" she said, and Mrs. Baysley repeated her refusal, sinking down again into her chair without taking America's hand. "I wanted to see your father," she said, and I was afraid Miss Ralson would resent her bluntness, but she only answered, still more gently, "Father isn't up yet, and he doesn't like to have us call him. Wont I do?"

Mrs. Baysley didn't say anything, and for awhile I did not see that she could not say anything. America poured out a cup of coffee, and went with it to her, and this time she did not refuse it. She put up her veil to drink it, and then I saw that she had been crying. She drank the whole cup off, and America

went and got it from her, and sat down again, and
waited patiently. It seemed a long time, but I do not
suppose it *was* long, before Mrs. Baysley spoke again.
She cleared her voice, and said, " I don't know but
what you'll do just as well. " " I'll go and wake my
father, if you are in a hurry, " said America. " No, "
said Mrs. Baysley, " I guess I'd rather talk with you. "
She stopped, and sat fumbling the paper in her hands ;
then she rose and came stiffly forward and laid it on
the table before America, and I could not help seeing
that it was a check, with Mr. Ralson's flourishing
signature.

America looked up at her puzzled, and Mrs. Baysley said, " I got it from Mr. Baysley, and I want you
to give it to your father, and tell him that we can't
keep it. We don't want to go back to Timber Creek
—at least the girls and I don't—and if we can just
go on here, as if nothing had happened, it's all we
ask. " " But didn't—wasn't the money coming to
Mr. Baysley ? " America asked, and Mrs. Baysley
shook her head. " There ain't any money coming to
us. " " But I don't understand, " said America.
" What should my father want to give it to Mr. Baysley for then ? " " I don't know as I can explain, " said
Mrs. Baysley, and she began edging toward the door.

" Maybe your father will tell you.   Any rate I've got nothing to say.   All we want is to stay on just as we were before.   We shall get through. "   She was looking down at the floor, as if she were ashamed of something, but now she looked up into America's face " I want to say that there are not going to be any hard feelings in us. "

America's nostrils puffed out with indignation in an instant.   " Any hard feelings!   Why in the world should *you* have hard feelings, I should like to know!   You have *him*, and I have *lost* him! "   Mrs. Baysley looked at her as if she did not understand.   Then she seemed to realize something, and she asked, " Hasn't he been here since? "   " Since? " said America.   " Since when? "   " Since he was at our house last night, " Mrs. Baysley said, and America flashed out, " Now you just sit right down, and tell me what you mean. "   " There ain't any call to sit down, " Mrs. Baysley said.   " He came over from the hotel where he says he is going to put up, from this out, and wanted to see Essie.   Well, *I* saw him, and I told him what she had agreed to tell him: that we did not feel he was beholden to her in any way or shape, and he was just as free as if he had never laid eyes on her. I don't know what fath—Mr. Baysley—would have said if he had been there, but he had come here to see your father, and I spoke for myself; and I told him we felt as bad as he did, and we didn't put the blame on him, altogether, if there was *any* blame, for we didn't believe he wanted to fool the child. She ain't anything *but* a child, anyway, and she's got chances enough to get over it. " Mrs. Baysley was winking hard as she said this, and she had got her hand on the doorknob, when she let drop the only bitterness that came from her: " Next time, I hope she wont be so ready to make a fool of herself because some simpleton is kind to her, and pets her up when he better keep his hands off. I wish you good morning. "

She opened the door and whisked out, and left America and me staring at each other. I don't know which would have spoken first, or whether we should ever have spoken again, if we had not heard Mr. Ralson behind us saying, " What's the row about! Who's been here, asking for me at eight o'clock in the morning? " America turned and pounced on him. " Father, what did you give Mr. Baysley this check for? " and she poked it at him. He looked at it with a kind of shame-faced smile, and she rushed on, " Was it to buy Mr. Ardith from him? " " Well, I shouldn't call it

that, exactly, " her father said.   I supposed you
wanted to make things smooth for them—it was nothing but a matter of business. "   " Oh, *business !* " she
flung out.   " You think everything is business! Well,
there are some things that are *not*. Mrs. Baysley has
been here to bring back your check, and give me Mr.
Ardith for nothing.   But I don't want him, and you
may have him, if *you* do.   Perhaps he'll sell himself
to you a little cheaper. "   She dashed the check at
her father's feet, and ran out of the room, and I could
hear her crying on the way to her own room.   Mr.
Ralson just said, " Well, I'll be damned, " and went
in to breakfast, and left me to pick up the check, and
put it into his desk.

Now, this is all at present, and I think it is enough
for one while.   I am finishing this, while the maid is
giving Mrs. Ralson her breakfast, and I have nothing
else to do.   I do not know whether to send it by fast
freight or not ; the postage on such a letter would be
something awful.   I suppose that I will let you know
the rest if anything else happens. I shall want to tell
it as bad as you will want to have me.

Your affectionate daughter,
FRANCES.

XLVII

New York, *March 10th., 1902.*

Dear Mother :

I almost wish there was no "rest" to the story I have been telling you, but things have to end somehow, when they begin, no matter whether you like the ending or not.

The worst of women is that they take things out in talk, and when they have said a thing they are just as well satisfied as if they had done it, and seem to think they have. I never respected any one so much in my life as I did America Ralson when she had that scene with her father about the check, and I would have done anything to help her in the stand she had taken. For once, I was proud of my sex, for although we can despise men easily enough, it is not quite so easy to honor women; and I did honor

278

her with my whole heart. She could not have taken Mr. Ardith back, under the circumstances, and kept a solitary rag of self-respect, and I gloried in her.

I did not see her the whole morning, and I had to lunch alone. About four o'clock this afternoon, she sent for me, and we had a long, splendid powwow. I never supposed she had such a clear mind, but she must have been thinking the whole affair over, and she was so logical that I could hardly believe it was the same harum-scarum person. She went over the case with me, from the time Mr. Ardith first appeared here, broken hearted from the way Miss Deschenes had used him in Wottoma, till he was taken down with the grippe there at the Baysley's. She tried to do him justice at every step, but her conclusion was that he had been wickedly weak, if he had not been simply wicked, and that no girl could be happy with a man she could not look up to. She said that he might have done much worse things, and still kept her respect, but she could not respect a man who was so afraid of hurting people that he could not say his soul was his own, and really did more harm by his shillyshallying than if he had taken a thoroughly selfish course throughout, and been guided by nothing but his own interests.

When I defended him a little, and said that I
thought he ought not to be punished for the harm he
had not meant to do, she said she was surprised at
me, and she argued me out of it. She declared that
if there was any such thing as justice, it had to be
blind to everything but the facts, and could not have
anything to do with the motives. She said, "Don't
you see that if I took Mr. Ardith back now we could
never look each other in the face? We should always
be remembering what had happened, and I should be
thinking how he had been feebly led away by his
pity, to let that girl get in love with him; and he
would be thinking how I had let my silliness for him
overcome my better judgment. No, there is just one
thing for it. We are parted now, and we must stay
parted."

She said a great deal more, but it always came to
this, and every now and then she would throw her
arms round me, and cry, and make me promise never
to leave her, but take her out to Lake Ridge, and we
would start a grape farm together; we could make it
pay by raising the early kinds, and getting them into
the market before anybody else. She made me want
to laugh, at times, but through it all, I honored her,
and she talked herself quiet at last, and said she had

not felt so strong in her life before. She kept up splendidly, that whole evening, and through the whole of Saturday. We went to a matinée, where there was rather a lovesick play, and she criticised it unmercifully; I never heard any one so funny about the plot, and the idiotic lovers. She would not let me go home in the evening; I slept in her room with her, and we talked till nearly morning, about all sorts of things, but mostly about girls and the kind of men they had married. She wanted to know if I had ever been engaged, and I tried to give her an idea of the kind of men I would have had to be engaged to in Lake Ridge; and she said that was just the place where she should like to spend the rest of her life, and not see another man to speak to as long as she breathed.

In the morning we went to church, and in the afternoon we talked again, and she made me say that I would write to you, and ask you if we might come out for a few days' visit this week; but I don't think you need get the spare room ready *just* yet. Suddenly, when she had arranged everything she said, "Don't you think its rather queer he doesn't write, and ask if he may come to see me?" I knew who *he* was, but I thought I would make her say Mr.

Ardith for the discipline, if her mind was veering
round that way, so I asked whom she meant, and
then I suggested that perhaps he was waiting for
some sort of sign from her. She was very haughty
at the idea, and said he would have to wait a good
while, and then we branched off on other things, but
in the midst of a discussion of Mr. Binning, and
whether it would be much out of our way to go round
by Boston when we went to Lake Ridge, she broke
off with, " I'll tell you what: if Mr. Ardith calls, you
shall see him, and give him his letters; I've got them
tied up. And I want you to put on your frozenest
Lake Ridge behavior, and let him feel that you are
handing him a small cake of ice from me. Will
you ? "   She began to laugh, and I did not know
what to make of her, when she said, " If he is anything of a man at all, he can't let the thing drop just
at this point; he *must* try to see me. I hate a boyish
man. I believe if I ever marry, it will be somebody
like Mr. Binning. A girl ought to marry somebody
who can understand her, or at least analyze her, and I
am sure he could do that. I wonder how I would go
down in Boston. I believe I could get him if I tried,
and I have got half a notion to try. It would be fun
Yes, I am going in for Mr. Binning. "

She ran out of the room, and when she came back, I could see by her very bright-eyed look that she had been crying, and then washing away the tears. She said, "I have decided to send Mr. Ardith's notes to him by a messenger, as soon as I know his address. I never want him to darken these doors again." She had hardly got the words out of her mouth before we heard the scraping of Mr. Ralson's latchkey, and then the opening of the door, and his saying, "Oh, come in, come right in!" and before I knew what I was about, he came in to where we were sitting, with Mr. Ardith by the arm. I expected to see America get up, and leave the room, and she did rise and stand looking at him magnificently, so that I should have thought he would have quailed at her glance. I don't know exactly how people *do* quail, but if it is anything like getting down on the carpet, and crawling round on their hands and knees, Mr. Ardith did not do it. He just stood with his head flung back, and gazing at her with such an appealing look that I was glad I was not in America's place. As it was I was perfectly dazed, but I managed to hear Mr. Ralson saying, "You come in here, and take a letter, Miss Dennam. Wallace, you'll have to excuse me a minute," and we left the two standing there together.

This was all I could write last night, for Mr. Ralson really had a business letter to dictate, and a pretty long one, which he wanted me to write out after I had taken it down in short hand, because he did not want the hotel type-writer to see it, even if she had been on duty, Sunday night. He went in to Mrs. Ralson's room after I had taken the letter, and I was scribbling away at the long-hand copy of it, when I looked up, and there was America standing at my side and smiling down on me, but looking rather silly. She flung her arms round me, and hid her face in my neck, and kind of smothered out, "He is an angel! But don't ask me, now!"

Of course I have heard since *why* he was an angel, but I guess you will have to wait till you see me before you find out. There are some things so sacred that they make you sick. But if those two simpletons were fated to come it over each other, they have done it, and they have done it whether they were fated to or not. What I am now trying to do is to untangle my own ideas, and get the rights of it, somehow. It is straight, about America. She had to go through that humbugging with me for the last three days, because it was our woman's nature to; but it is not straight about Mr. Ardith, and I am

tempted to go back to my original opinion of him as
a poor thing. Other people's forgiving him and re-
leasing him from the consequences of what he has
done, has nothing to do with it; that does not change
it, or lessen his responsibility in the least. The cold
fact is that out of his weak pity he let that silly child
get in love with him, when he was not only not in
love with her but was actually in love with somebody
else. That is what I cannot excuse him for, though
to be sure he has not asked me to; and on the other
hand I have to ask myself how I should have felt
toward him if he had died from the grippe, there,
.when everybody expected it, instead of ignominiously
getting well and remaining on everybody's hands.
Should I have thought he had expiated his offence,
or doesn't death really wipe out a wrong? It does in
novels, but does it in real life?

> "The evil that men do lives after them;
> The good is oft interred with their bones."

That is what Shakespeare says, and Shakespeare
knew a thing or two, though he does not always
let on. Am I mad with Mr. Ardith because he has
made a farce out of his tragedy by living through it;
and, if I am, how much better would the tragedy
have been? And is he responsible for the harm he

did not want to do, and did not mean to do, or was that just fate? If it was, what becomes of the suffering of that girl's heart that he let trifle with itself? Of course she was very young, and she will get over it; her own mother says she will. But does her mother really believe it, or does she say so because she is poor and the Ralsons are rich, and she does not dare to quarrel with her family's bread and butter? Any way, she seems to me the only one, except America, who is coming out of the difficulty with any chance of self-respect.

You see I am gathering up my principles from the woodpile, but they seem rather weather-beaten, and I don't know whether I shall be able to use them as effectually as formerly. Some of them are considerably frayed round the roots.

FRANCES.

XLVIII.

From WALLACE ARDITH *to* A. L. WIBBERT, *Wottoma.*

NEW YORK, *March 10, 1902.*

My Dear Lincoln:

I wanted to write you last night, but I was not equal to it. Since my letter of a week ago I have been through enough to try a well man, and I am not well, yet, by any means. But now I have something to get well for, and then I hadn't.

I went that night to the Baysleys', when I told you I should, expecting to see both of the old people, and tell them that it was off between America and me, and try to make it right with Essie. That is the brute fact; but of course I had got it into some heroic shape so that it was tolerable to the imagination. Jenny let me in, with her mouth pursed in hostility, and said her mother was at home, but her father was out, and she stood holding the door, so that I could go away if I chose. I said her mother would do, and in fact I

287

suddenly felt that I could manage better with her, for I always respected her more than her husband. I found her alone in the parlor, though I knew that Essie had just crept out of it. She asked me if I would sit down, and, country fashion, if I would let her take my hat; and then she left the beginning to me. I do not think she meant to make it hard for me, but that did not make it easy; and I fought away from it as long as I could. Then I found a sort of relief in facing the business. But it was an ugly business, and I cannot pretend that I put a pleasant face on it. She listened patiently enough, and then she asked me if I cared for Essie the way I did for America; and the fine pretences that I had been preparing turned useless on my hands. In the presence of her honesty I was obliged to be honest myself. I said, No, I did not; and then she asked why I had come back; was it because I had made the child think I cared for her, or because I thought she cared for me? That was a bad moment, Linc, and the best I could do was to hang my head. Then she asked me if I thought that was a good reason, and whether I expected her daughter to accept such an offer, or would I have wanted a sister of mine to do it? I had to own that I would not, and she said maybe I would consider that an answer ; she would send for Essie, and let her speak for herself, if I wished, after I had told her the same things. Silence might not have been the best thing for me, but it was the only thing, and I felt myself dwindling from a hero and martyr into something so infinitessimal that there is no name for it. That was when she began to have a little mercy on me, and to let me up from the dust. She told me that she had heard from Essie about our goings-on together, and that she did not blame me more than Essie, except that I was ten years older and knew more. She made a better defence for me than I could have made for myself, and she did not spare me her gratitude for what I had done for them in their sickness ; she gave me credit for good motives, which I will not pretend was not my due, though I could never have claimed it: but I know I was not selfish in going to live with them, and I did my best to help them in their trouble ; I see that as clearly as any one. After she had done that for me she signified, by holding her tongue, that I could go, and I went. I wonder I did not go through the keyhole; there would have been room.

I did not realize till afterwards that she had not said a word about America, and whether this was by accident or design, I could not help letting the fact praise her. I do not see how anybody could have done justice in the circumstances with greater dignity. She set me free, but she has bound me to her in ties which will last my life, and if ever the chance offers to do her or hers a good turn it will not be lost upon me. I have heard since that old Baysley had arranged it with Mr. Ralson that they were to go back on the same salary to Timber Creek, but Mrs. Baysley put her foot down on that. She and her girls have determined that they will stay in New York, and if any hint of their trouble gets home, it will not be through their bringing it.

I have written this out pretty squarely, and when I began, I thought I was going to tell you how I made it up with America. But it really made itself up; nobody had any sort of agency in it, and I least of all. Besides, I do not find it possible to write you the whole story as I intended, but sometime I will tell it, when we meet. I have talked every minute of my life over with America, and she knows just how unworthy I am. She agrees with Mrs. Baysley about me, but I guess she forgives me more because she loves me more.

Her forgiveness does not and cannot change the

facts, and I am not bringing to the happiness in store for me any overpowering sense of desert. I wish I could, for her dear sake, for she is worthy of unalloyed rapture. I feel that my ignominy is a sort of slight to her, but I cannot help it. To such a girl her love should be "one entire and perfect chrysolite," and I come clouded and fissured from an experience that I can never think of without shame. You can say I exaggerate, and I know that in a manner I do. But I am not wrong in recognizing that I have laid up for myself a life-long regret, which I may forget from time to time, but which, whenever I remember it, must be the pang that it is now. I forebode an inextinguishable vitality in the thing, and I know that in whatever happiest moment of the future I recur to it, the fact that I have *hurt* some one, that I have betrayed the creature that trusted me, that in my infernal soft-heartedness I have wronged the hope I inspired, will be a torture out of which the anguish cannot pass.

If you say I am not very well, and perhaps that I am looking at these things with sick eyes, I cannot deny it. I am not well yet, but there is nothing more serious than the cough that the grippe usually leaves behind it. There is talk of my going

South somewhere for that, and the talk is that I
am not to go alone.   But I will   write   you later
about that.

Yours ever,

W. ARDITH.

XLIX

From Mr. Otis Binning *to* Mrs. Walter Binning, *Boston.*

New York, *March 12, 1902.*

My dear Margaret:

I shall be glad to know, some day after we meet, just how a Boston woman so completely of our old tradition as you, should have allowed herself to become so absorbed in the loves of my wild Westerners. I could understand, of course, if you had met them in the fine ether of one of James's stories— I wish he still wrote about Americans—you would have been bewitched with his delicate *précis* of that affair; but not how you could suffer the affair at first hand, with the heat of their savage life in it: not merely suffer it, but long for it more and more, and heap me with reproaches for not satisfying your famine for it.

In each letter I have written you since my letter of the 23d February, in which I intimated a tragic

293

property in the situation, I have tried to feed your curiosity with divinations which I thought filling, but which you seem not to have found so; and at times your ingratitude has driven me almost to invention. The fact is I have felt myself becoming every day more peripheral to the situation. At the most I could catch a glimpse of its interior; I could chance a flying conjecture, I could seize a meteoric intimation, now from the secretary of the heroine, now from heroine herself. The heroine's father has been mostly in Washington; the hero has been safe from me in the hold of his grippe. What I knew, what I guessed, I generously shared with you; but I have too manifestly failed to appease your impatience. Now, when I come to you at last with the substance of the accomplished fact, I have reason to fear that you will reject it as gross commonplace, wholly unworthy of the fine issues promised earlier, and declare that I tardily bring you tidings which every one else that cares can know a day later.

Yes, Miss Ralson and Mr. Ardith are engaged: I do not know how, or when, or why. But she has told me so herself, in my quality of old friend: my date, if not the date of my acquaintance, justifies the phrase. They are engaged, and they are going to be

married, and going to the Bermudas: there is no
such desperate haste for their marriage, but the voy-
age is in the urgent interest of his convalescence, for
the grippe has left him with a cough, for which Miss
Ralson has heard that the air of those semi-tropical
islands is soveriegn; she is already talking of his
health as if she had been in charge of it for years.

They are not going to take the secretary with them;
she remains to console Miss Ralson's parents, and
she has been promised me for my own consolation in the absence of my lovers. But I do not
know that I shall outstay them here. New York will
be very empty without them. I cannot go back to
any pleasure in the Van der Doeses after the spectacle of this elemental passion; Prince Henry has gone
home, and there is little in the civic affairs of the
metropolis to entertain me. I have not yet decided
between the steamer for Liverpool and the train for
Boston; but if you do not see me soon you will hear
from me before you expect: one gets to Liverpool so
suddenly. Perhaps if I take the steamer I shall find
the Ardiths in Europe before I return; and I cannot
imagine finding them in Boston.

What I seem to see (with, I own, a somewhat self-
distrustful forecast) is the end of those social

ambitions, not very poignantly anxious, which have betrayed themselves to me in Miss Ralson. The house in the East side Nineties (have I never told you of that house? When I have been told so much of it!) will be built, but I doubt whether it will be made the basis of a more studied attack on the mythic Four Hundred: that poor Four Hundred which everyone who does not doubt it, abuses; and which has been driven to deny its own existence, by the intolerable self-consciousness created in it by the popular superistition. I hope rather that the Ralson residence may become the scene of those literary orgies which have been so lacking in New York, and without which it has been unable to realize itself a literary centre. I can imagine the energies of the young wife dedicated to culture in the interest of her young husband, and carrying him forward on the line of his aspirations with tireless devotion. The difficulty, if any, will be that she may not be able to distinguish between literature and journalism; in this she will be genuinely New York; and will conceive of accomplishing his career for him by making her father buy him a newspaper: say *The Signal;* I hear that her father already owns a controlling interest in it, and that Casman is merely his man.

I am not otherwise in the financial confidence of
the Trust, though since his daughter's engagement
has been announced to me—the events have necessa-
rily been prodigiously foreshortened in the brief time
allowed them—he has, as a parent, taken me to his
heart. After his daughter left us at dinner (which
we had in their apartment) last night he approached
the matter in a vein of jocose inquiry, and invited my
opinion of Mr. Ardith by the subtle generality that
these things were all in a lifetime. I ventured to say
that they were very pleasant things to have in one's
lifetime; and he rejoined to the effect that if Make
(so he shortens her name of America) was suited, he
was; and though it was rather sudden, it was the kind
of thing that would have seemed sudden, anyway.
He laughed with a great spread of his white moustache, and pushed me the whiskey, and began to
patronize me with condescensions suitable to a woman
of my years. He cannot make me out, I believe, but
these money-getters, though they are bewildered by
the difference of some other man, are never abashed
by it. I have no doubt but in his heart he despises
the fineness of the pretty boy, and hopes to coarsen
him to his own uses. The worst of it is that the fineness of Ardith will render him the easier victim;

money compels even the poetic fancy, and he will mis-
imagine this common millionaire into something rare
and strange, and of rightful authority over such as
himself.

But the daughter, who is of the father's make, with
the difference of "the finer female sense," may be the
poet's refuge. I will not despair for him; at least I
will not let you despair.

As you know I have sometimes had my misgivings
that their affair was not worthy of your interest, but
you have convinced me that it was worthy of mine.
These people whom it seems to have concerned less
intimately, who are as it were the material out of
which our romance has fashioned itself, have certainly
their limitations. They could not appeal to us from
the past or present keeping of our own lives. If they
were not so intensely real to themselves, they might
seem to me characters in a rather crude American
story. In fact are not they just that? They are
certainly American and certainly crude; and now that
they are passing beyond my social contact, I feel as
safe from them, and from the necessity of explaining
them or justifying them, as if they were shut in a
book I had finished reading. I am rather disposed
to rejoice that I have known them no more than I

have. If I could find the author I should like to make him my compliment on having managed so skilfully that he left some passages to my conjecture. What was the trouble, for instance, of my poor boy's—" half-broken and withdrawn "—that day in the park? What unknown shores of tragedy has not their story skirted in its course? Over what turbider social depths may not it have swum beyond my ken? Who was that mystical and subordinate second in his affections, if his darkling problem was one of conduct and not of art? Did it concern Miss Ralson, and if it did, how? I shall never know, and what is perhaps less acceptable, you, Margaret, never will, either

Your affectionate brother,

OTIS.

THE END.